Politics and the Anthropocene

Politics and the Anthropocene

Duncan Kelly

polity

The right of Duncan Kelly to be identified as Author of this Work has been asserted in accordance with the UK Copyright, Designs and Patents Act 1988.

First published in 2019 by Polity Press

Polity Press
65 Bridge Street
Cambridge CB2 1UR, UK

Polity Press
101 Station Landing
Suite 300
Medford, MA 02155, USA

ISBN-13: 978-1-5095-3419-7
ISBN-13: 978-1-5095-3420-3 (pb)

A catalogue record for this book is available from the British Library.

Typeset in 10.5 on 12 pt Sabon
by Fakenham Prepress Solutions, Fakenham, Norfolk NR21 8NL
Printed and bound in Great Britain by TJ International Limited

The publisher has used its best endeavours to ensure that the URLs for external websites referred to in this book are correct and active at the time of going to press. However, the publisher has no responsibility for the websites and can make no guarantee that a site will remain live or that the content is or will remain appropriate.

Every effort has been made to trace all copyright holders, but if any have been overlooked the publisher will be pleased to include any necessary credits in any subsequent reprint or edition.

For further information on Polity, visit our website:
politybooks.com

Contents

Acknowledgements

I wrote a first draft of this book during the late summer to early autumn of 2018, when the reality of global climate catastrophes and their uneven effects were a continuous presence. Seeing cataclysmic floods, tsunamis, wildfires and mudslides makes it very tempting to succumb to a basic fatalism about the capacity of politics to do anything meaningful in the face of such awesome natural power, or to an almost apocalyptic, dystopian fear for the future. Both responses might be justified, but if they are, they don't help much if what you're interested in is trying to see what your own research – in my case, the study of political thought and its intellectual history – might have to say about any of this. Yet surrounding these discussions of climate change and climate crisis, once you scratch beneath the surface a little, is a term of art that has been discussed for some time by specialists, but which remains still a bewildering one for a student of political thought and intellectual history to get a grip on. That concept is the Anthropocene, and its central suggestion is that human action has ineradicably changed the environment such that now it is impossible to say where 'nature' might begin and human action could end, so deeply intertwined are they. That makes it an eminently political problem.

My hope, in the brief compass of this book, is to try to show what sort of a perspective on the Anthropocene might be offered from the modern history of political and economic thinking, in ways that suggest something different from the wide variety of books already out there. And this is a book I would not have tried to write had it not been for the intense and intensely rewarding experience of teaching and working in the Department of Politics and International Studies at the University of Cambridge and of being a Fellow at Jesus College, Cambridge. My views about politics and political thinking have been profoundly reshaped over twelve years by my engagement with friends, colleagues and students here too numerous to mention. But for their specific help, support, advice, conversation, criticism and encouragement at various times over the short period of this particular project, and for pressing me always to try to be clearer about what I want to say about the Anthropocene, I am very grateful to those who have engaged with me directly, particularly Laura Díaz Anadón, Alison Bashford, Duncan Bell, Adam Branch, Stefan Collini, Shailaja Fennell, Jeremy Green, Hester van Hensbergen, Anton Jäger, Emma Mackinnon, Véronique Mottier, Renaud Morieux, David Nally, David Runciman and Helen Thompson. I also would not have had the temerity to begin writing on the subject had I not been fortunate to teach a seminar on the Anthropocene to sharply critical groups of MPhil students during early 2018 and 2019. Their willingness to think creatively about the issues really helped me to think about how this might be structured and argued. I am very grateful to them, as I am to my copy-editor, Justin Dyer, to Dave Prout for producing an index, and my editor, George Owers, someone whom I have known for over a decade, but with whom I have not worked directly on a book project before. His editorial interest and patience with my delays, and the (sometimes painfully) acute readers he commissioned to read through a still rather uncertain first draft, have been really helpful. Most of all, though, I remain grateful for the continued love and support of my partner, Rachel, and our son, Felix, to whom I dedicate this book.

Cambridge, UK
March 2019

Prologue
The New Political Times of the Anthropocene

The Anthropocene emerged as a concept within the fields of geological, atmospheric and planetary science. It did so as a direct response to the very obvious changes in climate that have transformed the ecology of planet Earth, and it affirmed that these changes have been significantly brought about by human activity. Putting human agency at the centre of geological and ecological transformation is at the forefront of debates about what the Anthropocene might mean, even if, at its most basic, the concept posits a deep and mutual interconnection between human activity and what was once called the natural environment. In this way, the Anthropocene is a concept for a world 'after nature', to the extent that it presupposes no distinction between human action and the natural world. Everything is connected in the age of the Anthropocene, an age that is said to follow from the relatively stable and temperate Holocene era of the last twelve thousand years. However, there is no scientific consensus about whether or not a new geological epoch exists, with clear stratigraphic markers in the multiple physical layers of earth, that could signify its emergence. Because of this, the Anthropocene remains a conceptual work in progress, argued about by human beings who are, in what is also taken to be indicative of the novel age of the Anthropocene, the first species to be self-consciously aware of their power in having transformed the earth. It is argued over too, because there is simply no way that such a transformative conceptual construction could ever plausibly seek universal assent. Concepts about the nature of human action are contested, and therefore straightforwardly political. They are always subject to deep disagreement.

This is a book on what some ways of thinking about the Anthropocene might mean for how we think of modern politics, and it approaches this question primarily from the perspective of the history of modern political theory. By so doing, I begin with an account of how the time-frames through which we understand the Anthropocene and modern politics might, and might not, intersect. From there, my argument considers the ways in which the various timescapes of Anthropocene time and political time pivot around several shared axes that have shaped the conceptual evolution of the Anthropocene. These cluster around energy and economic growth, population and inequality, indebtedness and questions of value. Tracing these overlapping concerns across the various generational time-frames through which each is configured, I suggest that the challenges of the Anthropocene for modern politics are twofold. In conventional terms, the Anthropocene forces politics to be more overtly ecological. By recognizing the deep interconnection between human action and the wider environment, the continued 'greening' of business, politics and policy, as well as the sorts of things debated at the level of the Intergovernmental Panel on Climate Change (IPCC), we can continue to pragmatically respond to climatic changes and allow for incremental planning into the future. A more radically 'Anthropocened' sense of politics, however, challenges the way in which we frame the terms of our engagement in the first place. For it suggests that in order to understand the ways in which our politics has come to be formed, we need to rewrite its terminology, its concepts, and thus its history, to show the interconnections between 'nature' and the 'artificial' world of politics. And if this is done, then it suggests the need to seriously critique our conventional thinking in relation to political values, economic limits, population growth and the nature of unevenly distributed ecological indebtedness. The challenge posed by the Anthropocene for modern politics is as much a radically humanistic one, that is to say, as it is a scientific or geological one.

*

Urbanization and the transformation of land use, particularly an increasingly industrialized agriculture, have wrought massive changes in the acidity of the soil and the oceans. The use and impact of fertilizers has vastly increased the emissions of nitrates and nitrous oxide, while the use of fossil fuels has contributed to the rise of carbon dioxide in the atmosphere. The resultant shorthand for many of these claims in tandem is that they have helped produce man-made, or anthropogenic, 'climate change'.[1] Moreover, they have done so to such an extent that these alterations in planetary atmosphere, sea levels and ice sheets, wind patterns and weather seasons, cannot plausibly be seen as being independent of human action. Nevertheless, rather like the way in which there are deniers, sceptics and proponents of the claim that human action has induced dramatic climate change, so too are there deniers, sceptics and proponents of the idea that underpinning such climatic shifts lies a new sort of Earth time, or geological epoch: the Anthropocene. And because there is no scientific consensus about this new designation, the concept has run free from its rather rarefied origins, and has been taken up by historians, social scientists and political theorists alike, eager to see what this framing concept might offer them.

Although there are threads and traces of earlier uses of the concept of the Anthropocene, it is really to Paul Crutzen, a Nobel Prize-winning atmospheric chemist, alongside Eugene Stoermer, a biologist, that we owe the contemporary sense of the term, and this was as recently as the year 2000.[2] The Anthropocene as a concept not only proposes a new stratigraphic era and negates the distinction between humans and the natural world, but, more pressingly, it opens up a new space for thinking about the connections between long-term geological or planetary timescapes and human or earthly time-frames. This is the sort of *deep-time* vision of the Anthropocene. Yet in its scientific ambitions, the Anthropocene simultaneously focuses attention on the way that human agency in the here and now might be able to consciously act to put a brake on climate change that was set in motion lifetimes ago.

For when Crutzen and colleagues first began to think about the possibilities of reverse geo-engineering the earth's atmospheric climate by, for example, cooling the atmosphere with sulphur to combat ozone depletion, they not only recognized the novelty of the epochal problem but also retained a sense of what human agency could do to act on nature. They had first begun to do so by contemplating the relationships between environmental catastrophe and nuclear fallout.[3] In turn, this has led many to think that the origins of the Anthropocene lie in the period since 1945, known as the Great Acceleration, and which produced the very real physical residue of man-made nuclear debris in the earth's soil and its wider atmosphere. This *accelerated-time* version of the Anthropocene suggests a new geological epoch alongside also a newly accelerating era, one in which the feedback loops from the deep-time origins of climatic change have begun to be felt in increasingly rapid and violent ways.

Between the deep time of the geological past and the accelerated time of the environmental present lies the *democratic time* within which the origins of the Anthropocene were first mooted. When Crutzen proposed the concept in print, he sought its original moment in the steam-powered industrial revolution of the 1780s, a period nearly coterminous with an age of revolutionary politics in North America and Western Europe that brought about the sorts of representative democratic politics we still live with today in large parts of the world. The Anthropocene, in an extremely confusing temporal way, connects all these different time-frames, issuing in what we might call multiple regimes of historicity, or ways of seeing what its force and content might be politically. It has become, that is to say, 'a way to understand the present environmental crisis in the context of deep time, the realms of the distant geological past'.[4] All this from a concept that had an early iteration in the 1970s and connected deep time to democratic time, but which gained renewed traction around the year 2000 and connected deep and democratic time with a newly accelerated time, and which has now been subject to a bewildering array of treatments.

This concatenation signals how much more than the merely geological or stratigraphic is at stake in understanding the Anthropocene. It might, in the words of one commentator, be better seen as a kind of 'epochalypse'.[5] The Anthropocene has indeed given rise to all sorts of fatalism – some optimistic, and some eschatologically pessimistic – about humanity and the end of a sustainable earthly habitat. Of course, the wide variety of meanings associated with the question of how to understand and conceptualize the actions of human beings and how their agency might have caused major climate change and transformed nature has been a major theme in environmental political thinking for a very long time.[6] In fact, the idea of a somehow 'separate' sort of wilderness or nature, out there in the world as something to be admired and protected by human beings, has long been debunked by environmental historians.[7] To my mind, the sheer variety of issues and temporalities the Anthropocene seems to encompass constitutes its major challenge, particularly if we are to try to clarify what it means for politics. Can modern politics be 'Anthropocened', so to speak, in order to take the measure of what sort of political futures are at least plausible scenarios for a new Anthropocene time? And if so, how might that be done? One of the most promising ways in which this might be accomplished is to configure the temporal perspectives of *deep time*, *democratic time* and *accelerated time* into the more generational time-frames of modern, particularly representative, politics. This might allow us to see the sources of our present concerns about the Anthropocene as distinctly connected to political and economic ideas, problems and projects, begun and considered in the 1960s and 1970s. If we ask which political and economic ideas, then, might most plausibly or prudentially have generational traction to make sense of an intersectional challenge like the Anthropocene across this generational time-frame and into our present, we might be able to get some intellectual control on such an otherwise apparently intangible problem.

Historians of political thought operate very broadly on this terrain, a field once famously described by John Maynard Keynes at the end of *The General Theory of Employment, Interest and Money*. Keynes portrayed a world ruled by 'little else' than the power of ideas, but the route

between the ideas of long-dead economists, philosophers
and 'academic scribblers', on the one hand, and practical
action in the here and now, on the other, is never straight,
but always crooked.[8] Those in power often distort and misdi-
agnose the texture and subtlety of the ideas they are using,
whether consciously or otherwise, so those ideas need to be
put into their own original context by historians of political
and economic thought if they are to be rendered sensible
in their own terms. But the power of those ideas is repurposed into new forms of 'worldmaking', or ways of framing
problems and issues, in each generation.[9] This is important
in the present precisely because of the distortions, reapplica-
tions, receptions, reappropriations, and so forth, that take
place. It is at this point that historians of political thought
also become contemporary political theorists, transitioning
between their concern with a sense of the past understood
one way in its own terms, to offer a distancing perspective
on how those pasts might become frameworks for understanding the present. Moreover, this allows us to try to
separate out the claims of environmental political theory or
the ethics of climate change from the temporal challenges
of the Anthropocene, and to see contemporary politics as a
particular sort of puzzle or predicament.[10]

In sum, this short book is really an attempt to show
some of the ways in which these new political times of the
Anthropocene can be explored with reference to debates in
the history of modern political thought that have evolved
since the 1960s and 1970s. It asks, more specifically, what
the history of recent political thought has to say about the
emergence of the Anthropocene and the challenges it poses for
modern, particularly representative, politics, and, conversely,
how the Anthropocene might challenge some of the conventional wisdom of that history. The much-vaunted 'shock of
the global' unites the political time and the Anthropocene
time of the post-1960s period, but in this book my focus is on
questions of temporality, growth and inequality, debts and
indebtedness, population futures and questions of value.[11]
Amid the wide variety of approaches to the Anthropocene
in the humanities and social sciences, few have considered
whether this sort of analysis might have anything to offer.
It is certainly my contention that it does, because historians

of political thought are used in practice to dealing with the multiple and overlapping time-frames through which ideas about politics, economics and the environment interact in both the past and the present, and how it is that from such complex historical and temporal perspectives we are best able to gauge how certain past ideas come to frame contemporary political debate. The challenge of the Anthropocene for modern politics, seen in this way, is not whether politics can 'save' the environment. Nor, as Jedediah Purdy has shown when writing about American environmentalism, is it to adjudicate upon whether or not modern democratic politics is specifically to blame for our current malaise, given its long, sordid and very well-known histories of exclusion, avoidance, violence and subjugation.[12] Recent assessments of the different dynamics through which democratic and artificial politics have intertwined with different visions of nature and of the modern, have made this very clear.[13] Perhaps unsurprisingly, then, one finds exceedingly similar arguments being made by writers thinking about Australia as much as America.[14] The real challenge of the Anthropocene comes in forcing us to confront how very difficult it really is to think politically at all across these competing temporal, spatial and intersectional perspectives.

1
Timings

Modern techniques and practices of government have been concerned with the effects of global warming, environmental transformation and sustainability for hundreds of years. In fact, modern representative politics and modern thinking about the environment and the space or territory where politics takes place, and the broader environment or climate surrounding it, emerged hand in glove. That we have been thinking about both for so long, though, often means that the temporal boundaries of how we think about their interconnections now tend to intersect and overlap with a great many other issues in our shared political imaginaries. So much so that it is hard to untangle the threads and traces. They form something like a dream world of complex representations in our minds, and they require something analogous to that which Sigmund Freud called a form of 'dream work', or engaged interpretation, in order to get straight what we're thinking about. This is even more necessary when we start to conider conceptual innovations like the Anthropocene, which threaten to destabilize our ways of thinking, often in uncanny ways.

Simplifying somewhat, it would not be wrong, though, to argue that the shared concern of modern forms of representative politics with environmental discourse emerged in earnest with the birth of political economy as a subject of inquiry.

This intellectual field first began to offer systematic reflections upon the relationship between global trade and commerce, and international war and peace. Would commercial interconnection and intercourse lead to peace, or was economic competition a form of war by other means, requiring new sorts of reasons of state underpinned by what David Hume called 'jealousy of trade'? Behind such visions lay claims about how best to maximize natural resources, husbanding them in ways designed to maximize comparative advantage, and how to really understand the centrality of climate to constitutionalism.[1]

This developed, particularly after the French Revolution, into a sort of environmental utopianism with the first so-called 'utopian socialists'. They considered novel types of administrative, cultural, spiritual and political forms of reorganization after the terror of revolutionary politics, and they presumed that part of their remit had to do with controlling the weather.[2] Forms of techno-utopianism and what we often call geo-engineering have been a standard feature of modern environmental and eco-socialist discourse ever since. Today, geo-engineering has many definitions, but the prosaic formula of the Royal Society captures the thrust of the issue, which is 'the deliberate large-scale manipulation of the planetary environment to counteract anthropogenic climate change'.[3] While technology makes new forms of manipulation possible, the principle of manipulation is, historically speaking, hardly news. If you're interested in managing or governing society, then managing the weather or your environment (given its importance to those resources you need in order to survive) is obviously a major issue in terms of thinking about your own political sustainability.[4]

Yet, in a different setting and several generations later, Russian scientists and French philosophers in the first half of the twentieth century began to consider the relationship between atmospheric systems and environmental collapse. They did so by considering both the ways in which the use of natural resources by humankind had profound atmospheric consequences, and how human consciousness evolved in collaboration with these wider features of life on earth. The pioneering work by Russian geologist and natural scientist Vladimir Vernadsky focused on what he called the biosphere (the sphere of biological life) and a related control system grounded in human cognitive capacities (what he termed the noosphere). His book on the subject was published in 1926. And together with Teilhard de Chardin and Eduard Le Roy, these figures of the 1920s and 1930s were foundational for the later developments in policy-related sciences concerned with human control of the environment.[5] At this point, human–nature relations were coming to be connected through the concepts of ecology, cosmology and consciousness. They would be up-scaled and redeployed in the post-war period in the form of systems theory, complexity theory, cybernetics and rational choice models of strategy, as ideas about environmental catastrophe, crisis and 'fallout' renewed their force upon human and political imaginations under the threat of potentially lethal nuclear annihilation.

If for Vernadsky, the noosphere was simply a stage in the development of living matter, it was one that rendered human action in the wider biosphere capable of changing, and therefore possibly even controlling, it. This was an important precursor intellectually to the concept of the Anthropocene today, as Crutzen well knew. The biosphere began to resurface in wider scientific discourse about policy in 1968.[6] But these connections had first been mediated by other Russian figures, particularly the mathematician Nikita Moiseev. It was Moiseev who adapted computer modelling and simulations of nuclear winter and environmental fallout in ways that were first shaped by this idea of a global biosphere that might, at least in theory, be regulated and controlled. And though these broader historical connections were hardly lost on Crutzen and Stoermer in the development of a concept that showed human transformation of the planetary atmosphere and environment, it was the possibility of changing the direction of travel by human control and regulation of these climate systems that they were increasingly keen to consider.[7] In fact, although the Anthropocene has become a counsel of despair for some pessimistic fatalists who fear that human beings can do nothing to offset existentially threatening climate change, for optimistic fatalists like Crutzen and others, things can always be changed if you can learn to manage the systems.[8]

The optimism of this science might very well overestimate its action-guiding force for global politics, but it certainly does stand in some tension with the often-pessimistic fatalism of much environmental political theorizing. However, both the optimistic and the pessimistic fatalistic registers leave little room for the anti-fatalistic sensibility that is at heart required for any plausibly democratic politics to retain its dynamism and avoid complacency. If an appropriately 'Anthropocened' politics is to avoid fatalism, it might have to consider the connections between Anthropocene time and political time a little more closely.

*

Unsurprisingly, the challenge of the Anthropocene for geologists and natural scientists has always been one of timing, but in their thinking about the emergence of a new time for the Anthropocene, they veer straightforwardly into politics. For example, in their provocative early formulation, Crutzen and Stoermer suggested that the real birth of the Anthropocene could be dated to around 1784, with the patenting of a 'parallel motion' mechanism in James Watt's steam engine.[9] The wider thought, of course, was that the advent of radical new technologies associated with the industrial revolution signalled a moment in which the imbrication between human agency and the natural environment took a new and more fateful direction. Industry and politics ran together. The problem, though, for a stratigraphic designation is that there must be a durable trace of this in the sedimentary layers of the earth, a version of the proverbial 'golden spike' that renders such a change visible.[10]

Although the industrial revolution was a revolution in the use and production of energy, the broader transition from a largely organic economy towards more mechanized and industrial production took quite some time.[11] Moreover, what stratigraphic trace in the sedimentary layers of the planet could the steam engine leave? In part, the answer to this lies with what steam power prompted in terms of a step-change in coal and fossil fuel extraction. This marked another level in planetary energy use, albeit unevenly distributed, and began the sort of transformation between human agency and

environmental change that could signal the emergence of
something akin to the Anthropocene.

In part, what flows from this looks like a version of
the argument presented in the schematic thesis of Daron
Acemoglu and James Robinson in *Why Nations Fail*.[12] For
these authors, political and economic success builds on
the positive feedback loops provided by 'inclusive' representative institutions for economic profit and advance, and
leads to early-adopter advantage, evidenced in the rise of the
Dutch and English empires. There are particular ironies for
the Anthropocene, however, when seen through this prism,
for the 'inclusive' institutions that bolstered rapidly developing empires and nations in the eighteenth century relied
upon massively 'extractive' practices of fossil fuel usage and
imperial conquest. And those residues continued to mark
the transition from coal to oil in many Western polities.
Energy-rich petrostates in the modern Middle East remain
affected by the extractive imperial powers that reset their
boundaries and political dynamics in the wake of the First
World War. And their massive wealth coexists with decidedly
extractive institutions, while 'advanced democracies' with
their avowedly inclusive institutions continue to benefit.

As political scientists have shown, natural resources can
often be a curse to those who are exploited, while resource-rich
countries can just as much foster the rise of democracy as they
can tend towards authoritarian or autocratic governance.[13]
For those who exploit these resources, whether in their own
territory or in the lands of those they have colonized, fossil
fuels and the capacity to extract them brought with them
the chance of incredible riches. The dramatic pursuit of oil
on the part of the victors in the First World War throughout
the Middle East, and in particular the gradual evolution
of American strategy in Saudi Arabia from a rather slow
beginning, have marked the geopolitics and geo-economics of
those relations ever since, in ways more obviously beneficial for
some than others.[14] What the history shows most obviously is
the centrality of carbon-related fuel and energy to the success
of modern democracy in the twentieth century, and its role
as a key driver of geopolitical conflict.[15] Indeed, Acemoglu
and Robinson also claim that 'extractive' institutional forms
(such as a hybrid state-capitalism model in contemporary

China) cannot generate consistent and long-term economic growth in the same way that liberal-democratic states can.[16] But such a binary is rather too schematic, and itself forecloses the thought that alternative ways of doing democratic politics with a modified growth regime might be possible, or effective.

If oil is the energy regime upon which much Western representative politics rests today, steam and coal were the original energy foundations of the *democratic time* of modern politics and therefore of the Anthropocene. Together, they signal two important facets of the concept of the Anthropocene for my purposes. First, they reiterate the claim that energy is a necessary component part of thinking about how our own politics, as well as our planetary environment, came to take its current forms. It is impossible to imagine the rapid success of modern representative democracy without the energy regimes that have helped it function, the infra-structural revolutions in transport and communications they underpinned, and without which societies governed by repre-sentative democracies would surely never have achieved such wealth as they have.

Second, this relationship between energy, activity, profit and politics coincided with the eighteenth-century emergence of modern representative and republican political regimes. These regimes were initially premised on ideas of active citizenship as the prerequisite for basic political equality under hierarchical forms of representation, alongside the upholding of a republican presumption that property, wealth and power tend to be coterminous. That signalled a disconnect between political equality and economic inequality that has not yet been resolved.[17] Their emergence nonetheless set in motion a series of arguments and struggles over inclusion, cooperation, property distribution and the sharing of risk across societies with both public and private credit that have formed the basis of the kind of representative politics we still find throughout the so-called 'global North' today.

Without saying more, if these connections hold firm, then the emergence of the Anthropocene, the rise of modern industrial capitalism and representative democracy seem coterminous. Anthropocene time and political time are the same time, and if the Anthropocene offers a particular challenge to contemporary politics on these fronts, it must be

to force it to confront the ways in which its pasts are necessarily inscribed upon its present.

One way in which this then overlaps with mainstream
debates in political theory is through the history of representative democracy. Out of the late eighteenth-century
revolutions in America and France, modern representative
republics emerged that were grounded on the idea of popular
sovereignty, but governed through representatives who acted
in the name of the people. These representatives, by virtue
of their position within a new conceptual amalgamation
of the modern 'nation-state', formed part of the idea of the
state as a sort of 'artificial' person whose agency could be
'represented' by a kind of fiction. Untangling the deeply
Hobbesian roots of this compound has motivated much
of the more recent and interesting discussions in modern
political theory, at least since the vogue for methodologies of
contextualism began to be pioneered in the 1960s and 1970s.
This is so particularly for the ways in which the abstract
sense of the state as an artificial person or entity makes clear
the connections between the origins of the modern state as
an artificial person, and the equally artificial personality of
corporations, particularly those (like the various East and
West India companies) that acted analogously to, or as arms
of, their states overseas. It further amplifies these connections by showing how both are, thanks to this artifice and
legal fiction, in principle eternal political entities. Unless
challenged, defeated, overthrown or destroyed, states do not
die 'natural' deaths, and in fact their responsibilities live on
after their temporary leaders and representatives have passed
away. The issue of debt and repayment makes the point most
obviously. Even when regimes change, debts are still owed,
and it is not normally the people of a country who are sought
out to repay their creditors, but rather their state, state banks
and state representatives.[18]

My point here is nevertheless simpler than this complicated intellectual history. It is just that one of the things that
modern representative politics permits, and what makes it
more adaptable and also messier in the face of the many
challenges it faces, is the distancing it produces between
rulers and ruled. Often noted as a major worry confronting
the liberty of the moderns, as opposed to the ancients, such

a stewardship model of politics does of course have its dangers.[19] More mundane sounding but even more immediately consequential for many people's daily lives is the threat of elite capture by the moneyed and powerful, transforming an already unequal representative democracy into an oligarchy. When media personalities and property moguls can attain the highest office in the United States, it is unsurprising that many think the hollowing out of American democracy happened quite some time ago already. Whether this threatens the 'end' of democracy, as many people now seem to think, is a moot point.[20] But the temporal disconnect between expressions of popular will (in, say, elections or plebiscites, and through institutional structures like parties, through pressure groups or online) and the policy-making process (running from legislative representatives down to street-level bureaucrats) allows for people to change their mind, to reconsider, to tinker and amend.[21] Representative politics with this combination of active sovereignty and daily government is, as Max Weber reminded his readers a century ago, the 'slow, strong drilling of hard boards',[22] which is both its strength, and its weakness. It compels responsibility and takes time, making it slow to react, potentially lethally so in the face of major challenges such as climate change.

Similarly, the power of lobbying by energy firms in moulding political considerations about the validity of human-induced climate change as something for debate is well known, and a major cause of political inaction in the face of seemingly overwhelming evidence. The recent reaction (or lack thereof in much of the international press) to the most recent IPCC report, and its conclusion that we must keep global temperature increases to less than '1.5°C to stay alive', shows this most obviously enough.[23] But the late modern history lesson that democracy seem to tell itself is that everyday forms of muddling through have produced regimes that, when faced with crisis and shock, seems malleable and adaptable enough to keep trying alternative solutions to such crises until they are resolved.[24] Climate change, however, looks like one of those 'wicked problems' or 'hyperobjects' that are too big for politics to 'solve'. And once the question is posed this way, debate is already stifled. On the one hand, democratic representative politics is given a history wherein its very resilience under extreme duress is thought to prove it the most flexible, creatively adaptable form of politics with which to try and seek new paths through the climate 'epochalypse'. On the other hand, if human beings are out of time to deal with anthropogenic climate change in conventional ways, then perhaps we need a mix of authoritarian and technocratic rule to basically solve problems that we, collectively, are unable to agree upon a course of action about. Once we realize that climate change and the Anthropocene are not problems that admit of 'solutions', however, we can situate or fix the temporality a little more creatively, and perhaps see why it is so difficult to mobilize a political coalition to act even in the face of climate emergency.

Whichever way you look at it, the relationship between adaptability, capacity and institutional structure is part and parcel of modern representative politics, and requires a sense of competing temporalities that are simultaneously immediate, generational and distant. This in turn suggests a way of connecting it to the similarly complex temporalities of the Anthropocene. Many similar questions that arise about the future of democracy (its capacity for renewal; whether or not one should be optimistic or pessimistic about it; the adaptability mixed with institutional rigidity that offers an open-ended politics moving forward) are analogous to the challenges raised by the Anthropocene for modern environmental activism.[25] Both are matters of political judgement, and both are about the ways in which an understanding of temporality shapes our sense of the Anthropocene as a regime of 'historicity', one governed by complex relationships between past, present and future.[26]

*

If the Anthropocene combines very distant pasts and futures, alongside the contemporary and the generationally very recent, so too must any putatively Anthropocened politics. Both need to be 'timeful' in understanding these connections. Nevertheless, the temporalities of political pasts, present and futures do not necessarily align with the times of the Anthropocene, and this is where the conflicts lie as to how to think about both in tandem.[27] Put more simply, both politics and the Anthropocene have criss-crossing time-frames, each encompassing *deep time, democratic time, accelerated time* and even the daily round of *news time*. Confusingly, however, they rarely intersect in the same ways. Instead, rather like the best analyses of climate change, which take seriously the reality of fundamental uncertainties about parameters, there are a diversity of meanings around both politics and the Anthropocene that make both more of a predicament, than anything with a purely technical solution. As Michael Hulme has argued, climate change is 'not a problem that can be solved', because at root it is an 'imaginative idea', encompassing deep disagreement about what exactly 'climate' even is. By remembering that anthropogenic climate change was a 'relatively low-key issue' as recently as 1987, we could do worse than remember that politics and political judgement, as well as climate change and the Anthropocene, are all 'imaginative ideas' that need to be understood in contexts, with their own perspectives or temporalities.[28]

Both political time and Anthropocene time are nevertheless concerned with the speeding up of our present, thanks to human action. For theorists of history such as Reinhart Koselleck, this was another part of a process that began in earnest in the middle of the eighteenth century, in a period from 1750 to 1850. This he called a transitionary 'saddle' period, or *Sattelzeit*. Then, time seemed to accelerate because events and actions could no longer be perceived in terms of the authority of the past, and politics could not be justified with reference to tradition or divinity. New conceptual evolutions such as 'revolution', 'class' and the 'state' charted these changes.[29] Simultaneously, history itself became something akin to a continuous iteration of novelty and change. Koselleck conjured new framing devices to understand what he called the relationships between the different spaces of experience that made sense of time, such as the 'horizon of expectation' (*Erwartungshorizont*), 'timeliness' (*Zeitlichkeit*) and the 'temporalization' (*Verzeitlichung*) that connects different dimensions of past, present and future, particularly via the concept of utopia. He did so in his own time, which saw the first outlines of the 'Great Acceleration' during the Atomic Age. But his awareness that the construction of historical distance was a necessarily artificial and conceptual endeavour, a way of trying to understand the temporal connections between past, present and future, emerged from his thinking about the earlier *Sattelzeit* in terms of the nature of the Enlightenment and the rise of modern Prussia.[30] What this illustration shows is that one challenge of the Anthropocene for modern politics is how to bring *deep time, democratic time* and *accelerated time* to bear on the more mundane time-frames of politics such as electoral or news cycles and leadership bids. It requires us to change the horizons of expectation and the temporalizing of politics in dramatic and unusual ways. By making deep time political in ways more recognizably tangible, the Anthropocene has in fact helped reorder our sense of the scale and temporality involved in political choice and calculation.

If Anthropocene time began during the *Sattelzeit*, it becomes a problem *of* modern politics and history, running alongside it from the beginning. Yet because it has only relatively recently been recognized as a challenge, it is a problem *for* modern politics and history too. Not only was anthropogenic climate change relatively low on the agenda in the mid-1980s, but the rapid rise of public awareness around it had much to do with clear and tangible instances of climate transformation (most literally a hole in the ozone layer above Antarctica) being considered in the context of wider socio-economic dynamics of inequality, poverty and the framework of 'sustainable development'. From the Brundtland Report in 1987 (where sustainable development was defined as development that 'meets the needs of the present without compromising the ability of future generations to meet their own needs' within the confines of technological capacity) to the first Rio Summit in 1992, the co-constitutive relationship between costs and benefits across socio-economic and environmental issues has become mainstream.[31] Yet although the initial periodizing of the Anthropocene by expert opinion nearly twenty years ago was to push it into the eighteenth century, and although initial reactions to that proposal quickly pitched for an earlier iteration running alongside the rise of agriculture and the birth of agrarian statecraft in the early modern period, now there are at least two other major temporalities in play around Anthropocene time.

*

Since at least 2005, an alternative genealogy has emerged to connect Anthropocene time to the period known as the 'Great Acceleration' after 1945. Here, the stratigraphic evidence is more direct. The detonation of nuclear weapons in the Pacific left obvious traces in the earth and its atmosphere. It was, and could only have been, an action undertaken at that time by human design, and it signalled a major advance in the increasingly rapid evolution of human capacity to alter the physical environment. And this *accelerated-time* moment reiterates the interplay between thoughts of environmental catastrophe and nuclear fallout in one direction, while the focus on acceleration also hints at the still further speeding up of the process of the dissolving of distance and time, which would later come to be the hallmarks of what is routinely called 'globalization'.

The echo of and allusion to Karl Polanyi's 1944 book *The Great Transformation* is no accident.[32] That book focused on the ways in which state boundaries and political-economic strategies often rebound upon one another with a sort of 'double movement', leading to unintended consequences. Polanyi's was a political economy version of complexity theory and systems analysis. His examples included the idea that liberal free-trade models of political economy sought to open up areas of commerce for wider profit and the promulgation of liberal values, but ultimately led to rampant anti-liberal criticism from ideological extremes when liberalism and parliamentary democracy were under siege after the First World War. Simultaneously, the obviously anti-liberal qualities of colonial rule were straightforwardly used by anti-colonial writers and critics of Western liberalism, whose crisis was then described as being of its own making. That was a strategy both of shaming oppressors at the level of theory versus practice, and of noting the obvious boomerang effect that the moral hypocrisy of 'civilization' as a metric of justification would bring about from those subject to its inequalities and injustices. W. E. B. Du Bois's editorial analyses of the First World War, or Gandhi's analysis of self-rule, are only the most obvious and best-known examples of such double movements in these early iterations of accelerated time and imperialism in the twentieth century.[33] But the colonial pretensions of modern liberalism and its anti-colonial critics are more than merely historical period pieces in the accelerated time of the Anthropocene. They form a past whose legacy still needs to be incorporated into the regimes of historicity that govern representative politics and its own sense of the past. From educational reform to acknowledging the debts owed to those who were colonized and exploited in a moment where political time and Anthropocene time have come together in the accelerated time of the post-war world, decolonization is still, as Frantz Fanon declaimed in 1963, a dangerous and violent business. That's because it 'sets out to change the order of the world' and the sorts of intellectual constructs that underpin it.[34]

As I have already suggested, many scientific writers considered the interplay between political-ecological and nuclear strategy since 1945, and in her pithy accounting of some of these moments, Jill Lepore reiterates these connections between environmental crisis and nuclear winter. The terminology of 'fallout' and 'survival' overlaid both.[35] Immediately thereafter, theorists of transactional games and strategies pursued these problems across research agendas driven by the needs and demands of the Cold War research university in the United States, helping to construct ways of seeing political choice that were stark, simplistic and extremely powerful ideological weapons.[36] At the same time, major émigré figures from Europe joined with the US government to pursue the thought that strategies of 'militant' democracy, anti-fascism and anti-Bolshevism, as well as techniques of dictatorship, psychological warfare and propaganda, needed to be understood if democracy was to defend itself against its foreign and domestic enemies.[37] Pursuing relationships of 'containment' that could effectively neutralize threats by pointing to the near-certainty of mutually assured destruction in terms of nuclear weapons, dovetailed with the near-impossibility of ever fully knowing the intentions of another person or political community, and both prompted questions of how to understand rational human action. One-shot prisoner's dilemma games are those where you tell the truth, keep quiet, cooperate with or sell out your partner (defect) for a better deal for yourself if the two of you are caught committing a crime. But you don't ever know what your partner will do. This lends itself to an obvious payoff matrix through which to think about rational choices under fixed conditions of uncertainty, resulting in the conclusion that it is always rational (in terms of self-interest and receiving with certainty the least possible penalty) to defect in a two-person, one-shot trade. This is so even though mutual cooperation would be better for both players. (By cooperating, you would receive a lesser sentence.)[38] It is only ever rational to defect, though, because you do not know how the other person will act in light of what you do. The assumption is that each person will seek their own best interest without any regard to anyone else.

However, once things are rendered more complex, whether in iterated games and scenarios, or (one might say) in the real world that real human beings actively inhabit, anywhere where strategy is involved across more than one decision point, it is clear that epistemic and interpersonal uncertainties about what to do and how to think about other people's intentions and actions become infinitely complex. They are subject to myriad interpretations, like a joke that never ends – I know that you know that I know that you know, but if you know that I know that you know that I know, and so on, things loop around in an infinite regress until someone says let's call the whole thing off. Any action might well be undertaken with reference to interpretation of what you think others will do, but you can never know with certainty what they will actually do; similarly, they will be wondering the same, and each iteration of an action or option choice or scenario can have various sorts of justifications at the level of morality, rationality or some other kind of criteria, but it can never be understood with certainty. Politically, this leads to a radical scepticism about the possibility of ever acting strategically with clear direction and certain expectation of results, or of explaining political action and political concepts at all without an awareness of their historical development.[39] It means there are no universal truths about political action, beyond the mere bagatelle of a *House of Cards* mantra that politics is always about the acquisition and maintenance of power. Even here, though, the only thing certain about political power is that there will always be unintended consequences to its strategic use.[40]

Given this combination of strategic uncertainty, atmospheric degradation and a global politics of containment, strategists and planners focused on how to consider forecasting and making provision for the contingencies of nuclear fallout and environmental catastrophe while trying not to bring them about.[41] The dangers were clearly real, and worries about the literal as well as the atmospheric fallout from nuclear weapons had been ongoing since atomic bombs were dropped on Hiroshima and Nagasaki in August 1945. Everyone knows about the doomsday clock, which began at seven minutes to midnight in 1947, and which in 2018 stood at only two minutes to midnight. The 'ticking time-bomb' threat has not receded very far from our political imagination, particularly when we consider the types of personalities who have control of the nuclear buttons, and set them against the structures that were once designed to constrain them. Those structures have routinely divested themselves of responsibility for politically rather self-interested reasons.[42]

Out of these earlier moments, though, Harry Wexler's weather experiments began to consider ways of controlling and measuring the climate anew. Equally, as the Cold War funding of think-tank policy entrepreneurs like RAND developed apace, their 1953 'Sunshine Report' about the relationship between atmosphere and radiation from nuclear weapons was another major turning point in seeing the atmosphere as part of a broader set of systemic relationships that could be used politically, and adapted.[43] Such connections helped to curate and cultivate groupings of seminars, scholars, teachers and proselytizers in what some have referred to as the variously 'interstitial' spaces in-between the conventional channels of academic or policy-related work.[44] The study of climate and environment encompassed a dizzying variety of specialisms.

In fact, the pioneering mathematician and theorist of games John von Neumann was already wondering in 1955 (from his position at RAND) whether or not climatological science might be the foundation of the newest and most insidious forms of warfare, presaging the formal elaboration of 'nuclear winter' a generation later. He was thinking first of the wholesale human transformation of the entire planetary environment, not merely the use of nuclear weapons to destroy the strategic resources of a conventional army. As we ask now, more often about rogue states or individuals who might get hold of 'dirty' bombs or use forms of AI and cyber-warfare to threaten a globally networked series of systems, von Neumann asked then: 'Can we survive technology?' His answer, in *Fortune* magazine during the mid-1950s, seems to have been a tentative yes.[45] And by the time someone like Carl Sagan became the public face of this thinking about human agency and the future of the planet amid geopolitical standoffs during the Reagan years, it had clearly been on the agenda for a long time.[46] Equally, the wider context of strategic uncertainty also helped give new motive force to the rise of a certain sort of monetarist and neoliberal project to reform political economy.[47]

Contemporary analyses of neoliberalism keep changing the temporal as well as geographical scale through which we might hope to see its impact in our present, mostly by rethinking its twentieth-century history. So too has the Anthropocene challenged the way we think about the relationship between the 'artificial' world of politics and the 'natural' environment since 1945. Environmental historians routinely track the origins of a serious concern with *the* environment as a singular entity back to a book by William Vogt, *The Road to Survival*.[48] It was written in the aftermath of the Second World War, when thinking about the future in terms of the existence of a single world environment as a system began to emerge. Many political theorists who confronted these spectres of nuclear war and environmental threat wondered whether the sorts of 'values' and kinds of politics that existed in the present could be safeguarded into an uncertain future. Perhaps they could by means of legislative provisions for a sort of 'constitutional dictatorship' pre-committed to democratic politics and liberal government, for instance, in the wake of an attack or some sort of existential threat.[49] For if politics could be safeguarded, then perhaps the environment could be too.

In thinking about these tangled historical connections between accelerated Anthropocene time and political time, there are still other shifting narratives here, leading some to see the imbrication of human action and the natural world in other ways with markers set much further back in deep time. *Democratic time* connects representative politics with steam and coal power, and more recently oil power. It presumes not

only a narrative of technological advance and the victory of
democracy as a political form, but also the realities of technological stickiness and infrastructural inertia, which render the
capacity to act upon such issues as climate change particularly difficult. Thereafter, *accelerated time* connects politics
and the Anthropocene through nuclear strategy and environmental fallout in a globalized world. Now we must also think
about the *deep-time* Anthropocene argument, which runs in
radically similar and also radically different ways.

*

Over the last forty years, scientists have continued to learn
more about feedback loops and the unintended consequences
of human activity that is part of a climate history of the earth.
That history connects the earth to a still wider planetary
'system', one whose geological times and histories might
conflict with earth history, and even with the practices
of writing histories of the earth or the world that might
interpret them. Because of this accretion of knowledge and
its increasing complexity, it has become difficult to hold on to
any single-origin story about climate change, and therefore to
any single-origin story for the Anthropocene.

The most recent IPCC report suggests global warming is
'unequivocal and rapid', and that since the 1970s, 'most land
regions have been warming faster than the global average'.
Yet our sense of the tipping points involved in understanding
which particular results of climate change that began in the
past but which we are seeing in the present, makes it very
difficult to deal with. Even the language of what was once
thought of as progress, such that human ingenuity might
simply 'time-bomb' the future through the development of
synthetics, for example, has come back to haunt us, setting in
motion unanticipated changes to biological life on earth across
all species whose temporal dynamics and feedback loops are
extremely complex.[50] Moreover, once aligned to the target of
mitigation that requires keeping to less than 1.5°C change
going forward, this means that human beings have between
thirteen and thirty-two years to reach this target, assuming
the current warming rate. That rate in turn suggests a time-
frame of double this before stabilization occurs.[51] Within this

scientific presentation of complex temporalities and feedback loops, the authors of the IPCC report acknowledge four major asymmetries around meeting this target. These relate to the differential contributions that have brought about the situation the earth and its populations find themselves in; the differential impacts of action in the face of this situation now; the differential capacities to shape possible solutions; and differential future resource capacities. All of this amplifies the fact that there is a clear 'non-linearity' of risks and impacts associated with the time of the Anthropocene, to say nothing of the unknown implications of the sixth extinction and the human wiping out of seemingly 60% of animal populations since 1970.[52]

Small wonder that some people choose to trace the roots of the Anthropocene back much further than we have so far thought about, into a *deep time* of many thousands of years. If the onset of the Anthropocene is about human 'niche' effects, they could certainly be pushed further back into the Holocene, and there are lots of pseudo-mythological narratives around this origin story. In the best-known overstatement about this, the Anthropocene is the long-term result of the human capacity to make fire, making ours a truly Promethean fate. But as radical critics note, although this pushes the origin story some way back, it nevertheless reconverts the criss-crossing time-frames of Anthropocene time and political time into a linear or Whiggish narrative, where things couldn't be otherwise now because of primitive human effects then. An alternative deep-time version of Anthropocene time is a still longer geological prehistory of the present.[53] Focusing on human niche effects as tipping points simultaneously overplays the impact of certain sorts of human action while devaluing the autonomy of human choices in the face of evolutionary adaptive preferences to circumstances or structures somehow beyond or separate from their agency.[54] This is why, as Dipesh Chakrabarty explains, the time of the Anthropocene is at the same time both natural and artificial, combining the planetary history of the earth and its systems with the world history of its inhabitants across multiple and overlapping scales.[55]

In this, the Anthropocene remains both like and unlike the simultaneously natural and artificial realms in which politics takes place. In both cases, singular epistemologies about something so complex as either the Anthropocene or the predicament that is politics avoid registering two more interesting issues. First, the discussion of deep time and the Anthropocene is often structured like the conjectural histories of modern political thought that emerged in the eighteenth century. Then, conjectural narratives around the origins of justice, of language, or labour and political economy, or of the legitimacy of rule, worked back from some rather general premises (like the naturalness or otherwise of human sociability) to curate various stages or stadial dynamics in the artificial evolution of human attributes and institutions. The different ways in which these attributes evolved and developed required a sense of the importance of geography, climate, culture, economy and institutions. And that is what critics of the singular deep-time epistemology of the Anthropocene also want to bring back in their focus on the multiple and overlapping 'epistemic geographies' of the Anthropocene. Once that is done, we are forced to confront the combined and uneven development of the Anthropocene as part and parcel of the combined and uneven development of modern capitalism and modern democracy, and to reckon with the ways that imperial, colonial and extractive-energy regimes undertook historical injustices that are still inscribed on contemporary politics.[56] Moreover, apart from the 'natural capitalism' writers, who think otherwise, if capitalism cannot itself provide us with the sorts of profit rates that might make a business-led transition to a no-growth or de-carbonized economy plausible, it becomes very clear that the conflicting temporalities of politics and the Anthropocene under the current growth-, energy- and value-based assumptions of a global capitalist economy are a major source of the basic incompatibility between these different cycles.

Second, a linear deep-time narrative struggles to incorporate a sense of perspective that could make sense of our own politics. Indeed, when it comes to geological time-frames, putting the deep time of pre-Holocene eras into conversation with contemporary political time is at first very jarring indeed. Nonetheless, the conceptual terrain of the Anthropocene has itself altered over the course of a generation, and during that time we have learned yet more about the realities of what actually did happen at various points during these periods of deeper time, precisely because our scientific knowledge has increased. That process of knowledge acquisition about our past will surely continue, and therefore evolve to structure our knowledge about how we might think about the future as that future evolves. These developments have prompted, and presumably will continue to prompt, new environmental histories of hitherto well-known periods, such as the recent re-evaluation of seventeenth-century revolutions across Europe based on new climate-related data. This has allowed us more clearly to appreciate that in every epoch where we look for past evidence, there have been people who were worried about the threat to natural resources from overuse by human beings, and the 'shock' of the Anthropocene is little new in this regard.[57] Scientific advances have the capacity to render historical events more textured, or granular, and thus more instinctively as well as intellectually meaningful to us. At the same time, our sense of these overlapping histories exists as a combination of the 'horizon of expectations' that opens up into the future, and the 'spaces of experience' that new conceptions of history provide.

When the deep past is mined like this, it can actually have traction for the present. As past events in deep time are rendered more humanly intelligible, and as our sense of their causes, consequences and possible or probable re-occurrences in the future develops, we can think about how to act, or not, on that information. This is one of the two major challenges for conventional politics raised by the Anthropocene. The first is how to register the enormity of the implications of a transformation of natural or geological time within the artificial timescapes of modern politics. The shock of the Anthropocene, to the extent that it reconciles human agency and the natural world, means that 'natural' time can no longer be separate from 'artificial' political time, and that the connections between deep geological time and accelerated political time have to be brought into any overall assessment.

At the same time, as new understandings of the past open up new options for thinking about and planning for alternative political futures, the second challenge concerns how to act prudentially on the basis of this knowledge. And the most obviously prudential route open to us, if we are interested in keeping our political options open, seems to be to adopt an historically minded approach to the problem of the Anthropocene as a sort of imaginative work in progress. Then, we can begin to think plausibly about the sorts of futures that a transition away from the 'energy sources of the *ancien régime*' might presuppose.[58] This is, in fact, why the recent IPCC report is an exceptionally radical political document underneath its dry and sober presentation of data.[59] In this way, we might remember that vast questions about how to reconcile problems of planetary scale with political judgement are long-standing concerns for early but conjoined histories of climate science, the study of natural disasters, and the emergence of representative politics.[60] The current vogue for books about the ultimate extinction of humanity in an age of environmental catastrophe and automation can only build on such long-standing connections. They march in parallel with the swathe of studies about democratic death, dysfunction or simply disaffection which have appeared against the backdrop of late capitalist inequality and a rising sense of existential threats. All have to speak directly about how human beings understand the 'environment' in which they operate, because as an 'integrative object in its own right', the environment in which humans live has a history.[61] And the history of what sorts of limits there might be to environmental growth and change needs to be connected with broader histories of political and economic growth or change.

2

Ecological Inequalities

In the early twentieth century, concerns about the environment (or 'ecology') in which politics and economics took place routinely tracked intellectual and political conflicts between capitalist and socialist accounting, and the possibilities of economic planning. Unsurprisingly, these were debates that first really emerged in the wake of the First World War. Then, writers on both the left, such as Otto Neurath and Oskar Lange, and those broadly on the right, like Ludwig von Mises and Friedrich Hayek, developed competing arguments about the possibility or impossibility of economic and political planning, production, transfer payments and institutional designs, based on a shared understanding of the limits of human reason in the face of complexity and uncertainty. These shared worries about epistemic uncertainty amid information scarcity nonetheless hinted at the possibility that in principle, with enough calculating power (or, at the least, enough centralized political power), goods and resources could be allocated according to a different value system than that presumptively grounded on a 'free' market.[1] These debates reverberated across the twentieth century. Similar issues were replayed in the 1970s, for instance, in the short-lived cybernetic socialist planning experiment (known as Cybersyn) under Salvador Allende in Chile. From an operations room reminiscent of the bridge of the USS *Enterprise* on

Star Trek, networked computing power and cybernetic theory combined to use big data to distribute resources according to planned need. The radical experiment was quickly subverted by American industrial intervention from ITT and came to an abrupt end with the political assassination of Salvador Allende in 1973. Thereafter, a neoliberal 'shock doctrine' was imposed upon Chile as General Pinochet took power.[2]

At the same time, Marxist analyses of fascism, big business and the permanent arms economy of the 1960s and 1970s, as well as the anti-war movements across Europe, Africa and America, also fed into wider debates about political-economic ecology, though in an unorthodox way. These contexts compelled writers to think anew about the role of the state and its relationship to capitalism. And the relational theories of the state and state power that were developed then, and which continue to evolve still, offer something of continuing relevance to understanding political time in Anthropocene time. They show that although there are tendencies and constraints that determine state policy and real-world politics, there is nothing that necessarily points towards states *always* reflecting the interests of big business and capital.[3] Things can always be different.

In a wider public realm, there were clear echoes of earlier concerns about planning and information management in new environmentalist histories of the 1960s and 1970s that brought together concerns about the relationships between food supply, cheap energy, population and Marxist theories of capitalism's combined as well as uneven development.[4] Many of these were triggered by concerns about what we mean by economic growth and prosperity in the broadest possible sense, and by the 1970s, something of a paranoid-sounding style emerged to consider this in terms of energy, particularly the way in which energy use could only end with entropy. The earth itself came to be seen as an entropic steady-state organism, capable of irreducible, though not irreversible, outcomes and positions, such that there literally were worldly limits to growth. In this chapter, several of these various intersections between energy, information and economy are brought together under the broad heading of ecological inequalities. For the challenge of the Anthropocene here is a challenge about how we should understand the broadest possible ecological setting within which political and economic discussion might take place.

*

In 1955, the economist Simon Kuznets was developing his pioneering work into national statistics in order to determine what he thought to be a general trend across generations, periods he understood as around twenty-five years in duration.[5] This trend was towards increased equality of income, assuming a constancy of relative distribution and a narrowing of relative inequality. His work was the inspiration for more recent studies of inequality by Anthony Atkinson and Thomas Piketty, and although the data sets have expanded and the techniques for assessing them have increased in sophistication, the basic contours of Kuznets's account remain powerful. In part, this is because he recognized that over the long run, those trends can easily move in opposite directions, and the only thing that puts an enforced brake on increasing income inequality are political decisions which reject the presentation of such inequality as 'natural'.

As Danny Dorling has more recently argued in a book called *Do We Need Economic Inequality?* (spoiler alert, the answer is 'no'), there is nothing natural about economic inequality, and certainly nothing rational about the thought that, for instance, some people occupy such a role in society that their monetary value per hour is justifiably worth one hundred times that of anyone else.[6] What Dorling and others have shown is in line with most of what has become increasingly obvious as people have begun to rewrite the history of the Anthropocene to take account of combined and unequal development in the history of modern capitalism: that is, that a system predicated on inequality tends to naturalize artificial and political distinctions around class, ethnicity and gender, for example, and does so in order to justify rampant levels of exploitation across whatever frontiers or marginalized spaces it can.[7] Clearly there is nothing 'natural' about this at all, and histories of the ways in which forms of knowledge must first be represented and curated before they can become motors of historical and political change have long suggested as much.[8]

This is why scholar-activists from Naomi Klein and George Monbiot to Andreas Malm and Jason Moore explain the history of anthropogenic climate change generally, and the emergence of the Anthropocene particularly, as necessarily part of the history of capitalism, and therefore the history of economic growth and inequality. It is also why Marxist-inspired writers on the subject (as well as on much else besides) take the commitment to historicize everything absolutely seriously, to avoid the temptation of reifying or naturalizing what is in fact contingent and artificial. And because there is no 'natural' history to be had of such concepts and topics, they are always the subject of argument and conflict. So the non-naturalized history of the Anthropocene must be, like any other non-naturalized history, the history of arguments and conflicts over the terms that make it up. This basically Nietzschean point reaffirms that we should write the history of our moral and political concepts genealogically, seeking the perspectives that particular arguments offer us in terms of how we might see the world.[9]

There is an added edge to this for the Anthropocene. As Timothy Morton has put it in his book of the same name, human beings simply cannot avoid 'being ecological', because no one is ever disembodied or atomized such that they are separate from all other living things in the world. At the same time, there is no singular scale across which ecological questions can be dealt with. One reason for this has to do with the temporal disconnect between the cycles of political time and Anthropocene time as outlined in the previous chapter, which make it so difficult to imagine Anthropocene-relevant forms of political agency being either mobilized or represented, even in the face of a near-permanent state of climate emergency. Or, rather, there is no singularly human scale, which means that the idea of writing a genealogy of the Anthropocene as a form of political critique of the present takes on a sort of ecological imperative.[10]

For Morton, the Anthropocene poses a dilemma in that it is a form of the uncanny, at the same time both familiar and not.[11] This is made manifest for many of us by the fact that the environments we call 'home' are changing so rapidly because of climate change that even the idea of staying 'at home' or staying put no longer means a place where everything stays the same.[12] This is why Morton suggests that conventional styles of writing about ecological thought (the 'immersive', the self-consciously 'authentic', the 'religious' and the 'efficient') typically make a category mistake. By trying to denature the human from the ecological to make sense of how 'we' feel about the 'environment', they commit us to various anthropocentric fallacies.[13] In terms of the 'efficient' style of seeking solutions within current frames of reference, this also requires a sort of 'economentality', a way of pricing and evaluating the environment as something to be calculated, a form of political reason that developed alongside a justificatory commitment to carbon democracy, particularly in the form of oil politics, and which is so powerfully entrenched in our political imagination.[14] Being appropriately ecological for Morton, then, would certainly not mean breathlessly advocating for an environment out there that human beings should value and save in an overbearing or preachy manner. It might also mean being merely indifferent (which is to say, tolerant) towards other parts of this worldly ecology, while learning about what it actually entails. In fact, this has in fact been part of the wider project of ecological economics as it developed through the twentieth century, offering new perspectives on questions of economic growth and energy use by effecting a more holistic approach to the mutually constitutive relationship between economy and environment.

What does an ecological economics look like? In one way, that's easy to visualize, through the 'doughnut' economics recently popularized in public debate.[15] There is no spatial disaggregation of the environment that sustains human life either from the constituent parts of mainstream economic thinking or from the environment within which political or economic conflict takes place. Environmental economics, slightly differently, traces its origins back to the 1950s in America, coterminous with the work that Kuznets was doing. Then, the 'Resources for the Future' initiative was established in Washington to consider the stability of natural resource supply. In the 1960s, this quickly aligned with worries about environmental fallout and depletion, crystallized in Rachel Carson's *Silent Spring*.[16] Earlier still, in the wake of the First World War, technical debates around optimal use of resources, negative externalities (like pollution) and the relationship between national wealth and welfare had been pioneered by welfare economists in Oxbridge and London.[17]

In fact the history of ecological economics pre-dates its formal emergence in Stockholm around 1982. It was certainly present in debates about growth and even de-growth in the 1960s in France especially, and ecological economists 'probably regard environmental problems as being more serious than do environmental economists'. They focus more directly on the relationships between energy and ecology.[18] One of the pioneering historians and practitioners in this field, Joan Martinez-Alier, traced the contours of its intellectual evolution more than thirty years ago. He wrote a book that showed the utility of seeing economics from an ecological perspective, by considering the relationship between energy production and the exhaustion of finite resources as they become cheaper because more efficiently derived and used.[19]

Interestingly enough, Max Weber's critique of 'energy'-based (or 'energetic') cultural histories of socio-political change is one under-appreciated early moment in the evolution of this perspective that Martinez-Alier alights upon. Weber worried about explaining socio-political problems with reference to the laws of energy outlined by contemporary science, and through Wilhelm Ostwald's particular adaptation of contemporary energy physics. Ostwald suggested reading off social progress from the 'synthetic' amounts of energy used to produce 'general' forms of knowledge and laws. Weber thought this was an incorrect application of scientific argumentation to problems within a social realm, but it was nevertheless coterminous with his wider concerns about the fate of politics in a world where the last of the most important forms of fossil fuel energy had been used up by rapacious and competitively imperialist nation-states. In that world, it was capitalism that stultified the possibility of human and political freedom, and capitalism that fostered relentless energy competition.[20] This was a recurrent refrain for Weber, from his consideration of food, fuel and economy in the conflicts of interest between German and Polish labourers in the 1890s; to the final moments of *The Protestant Ethic and the Spirit of Capitalism* in 1904–5; into the First World War when writing about the fate of German politics and the relationship between parliamentarism and monarchical government; and right up until the end of his life when considering politics as a vocation.[21] After the war, Weber put his finger on the problem of coal and natural resources for modern economic growth and power, pointing to the energy dynamics behind the Versailles Treaty, and why the occupation and appropriation of the Saarland and the Ruhr were so important to understanding another swing in the pendulum of Franco-German grievance that dated back to the war of 1870–1.[22] Energy regimes based around coal also formed part of the political strategizing around Versailles of numerous other global players such as Japan and China, whose shared interest in the implications of the political decision to 'give' Jinozhou to Japan after the war became one proximate cause for the nationalist May Fourth movement in China.[23] This was how, for Weber, energy, ecology and politics came together in considerations of national interest.

Yet Weber's concern with the historical uses of energy and fossil fuels might also have developed through his reading and teaching of modern marginalist economists like W. S. Jevons. For it was Jevons's consideration of the coal question from a British perspective, alongside the elaboration of modern marginalism and its undercutting of Marxist economic theory, that Weber was most in sympathy with.[24] In fact, the deeper evolution of modern ecological economics is often thought to begin properly with Jevon's famous analysis of the coal question and British political leadership from 1865.[25] Coal was the foundation for rapid imperial profiteering and political expansion, but it seemed to be a finite resource, though not everyone thought so. In the generation prior to Jevons, some boosters noted that if there were nearly three thousand years of coal deposits left, there was no harm in trading on abundance today, because tomorrow was always far enough away. For those more conservatively minded, such as Prime Minister Robert Peel, some limits to exports might be prudent given the nature of carbon-fuelled competition between industrializing nation-states. This might require the husbanding of mineral resources in such a way as to fulfil the Burkean social contract between the generations past, present and still yet to come. What this meant in the early nineteenth century was that rapid expansion built on a finite carbon foundation had led to massive new consumption patterns, and those consumption patterns transformed the nature of the 'public interest'. Politicians had to reorient their political-economic choices to deal with the temporality of deep geological time and the fossil fuel economy, the generational time-frames of political competition, and the democratic time of politics more generally. Curating those choices as part of a political-ideological commitment to a certain vision of the national community still remains a major task for contemporary politicians in the age of the Anthropocene.

Then, just as now, these temporalities were in constant flux. If some thought the coal deposits of England could last three thousand years, others thought their lifespan nearer to three hundred years. Something like deep time and emergent democratic time were developing in line with the political economy of international competition in real time. And at the same time, a Malthusian worry about the relationship between population and food was being repurposed to suggest new technological and energy-based resolutions to this dilemma.[26] When Jevons's work appeared, his synthetic combination of Malthusian political economy with contemporary debates about geological time showed that not only did population rise geometrically while food production increased arithmetically, but coal consumption also rose geometrically. As it did so, increased consumption would decrease available stock at an ever-increasing rate, so that the profitable advantages from more sophisticated extraction techniques and rapid consumption would soon tilt from an optimistic future where coal helped provide the food that offset the Malthusian problem, and quickly turn into a pessimistic image of the destruction of resources and an irreversible cycle of decline. How this should be managed was the subject of massive public and political debate, and ultimately the politicians rejected Jevons's Malthusian pessimism. But what such debates highlight is that the pendulum swings between optimism and pessimism about markets, resources, technology and ideology are nothing new when seen through the prism of the energy-based ecological economies of modern representative politics.[27] In fact, and somewhat ironically, the original pessimism of the Malthusians often turned out to be the foundation for a wider social optimism because the shortage of resources routinely induced new forms of innovations just when they were needed.[28] In effect, technology comes to the rescue in the nick of time, but until that point, it might remain unhelpfully 'sticky' with reference to adaptability and demand.

Equally then, just as now, although there were options to deal with the decreases in consumption that followed from initial efficiency savings, the paradox to which Jevons's name would soon be applied was that these inefficiencies rebounded upon the state. The paradox involves the promotion of an increasing reliance upon particular fossil fuels, even though their extent is finite, particularly when the prospects of actually changing resources were uncertain. Oil was not much on the horizon when Jevons was thinking about this problem. Nevertheless, this forms a moment of decisive importance for thinking about a possible starting date for the Anthropocene. For Jevons, the evolution of steam power prompted the turn to coal to become more efficient and productive, and dramatically transformed the political and economic opportunities open to Britain. Modern democratic politics based on the energy of coal and steam fuelled the industrial revolution, which, even if it moved with a slower energy transfer than we often think, conjoined modern representative politics with the carbon democracies we have lived with ever since. And now just as then, we are faced with a dramatic choice which couldn't be put better than Jevons had it at the very end of his report on *The Coal Question*: 'We have to make the momentous choice between brief but true greatness and longer continued mediocrity.'[29] That is to say, there is a choice to be made between a stationary state to come, and the brief greatness provided by an abundance of energy that will later dim, because the physical fuel sustaining it just runs out. Does greatness require you to make the best of the resources you happen to have at a particular moment for everyone, or to pursue a Machiavellian politics of mastering fate or *fortuna* in a ceaseless world of energy competition?[30]

In an imperial context, the political choice that arose for Jevons was whether to go all in for jam today, so to speak, with little reference or care towards future generations in the knowledge that those generations would blame their predecessors for their failures, even if fleeting glory had been the result. Or was the prudent response to finite resource constraints to try to husband resources, and better the overall condition of the widest possible population in the present? That attempt might also end in failure, but one would at least be relatively blameless in the eyes of the future. In a post-imperial situation, where the balance of natural resources available are both greater and lesser simultaneously (often more efficiently extracted, but certainly less readily accessible), the old imperial idea of an Anglospheric union or trading zone based around shared cultures and resources has returned anew amid the collisions of Brexit and Trump in the Anglo-American world. More often than not, these just repeat racist hierarchies, so much so that no sane political economist today (though occasionally a perhaps slightly less than sane politician) would seek glory through the fruits of empire.[31]

*

In the 1970s, the multiple conjunctures of peak US oil production and the discovery of new fields in Siberia, British withdrawal from the Gulf states and the potential windfall of North Sea oil, as well as the increased power of OPEC, meant 'there was no way of guaranteeing a stable and cheap supply of oil' to Western economies.[32] When President Carter offered the crisis in oil and energy for the US economy as the 'moral equivalent of war', it seemed there was little irony in his reappropriation of phrasing first used in 1906 by the pragmatist philosopher William James. James had thought about the toughening up required of modern citizens in a world where the prospect of physical conflict was diminishing, but where effective preparedness of mind and body remained a pressing concern for a vibrant and healthy democratic citizenry.[33] Yet where Jamesian moral equivalence was designed to put individuals on the offensive, Carter's moral equivalence seemed to come from a position of political defensiveness. Since the mid-1970s crash courses in the geopolitics of oil dependency and independency, cheap oil and the possibility of energy independence in the US has become a live possibility once again. As energy economists like Dieter Helm suggest, a combination of fracking, a shift to electric energy and renewables, and the potential for both technological and democratic adaptability signals the real possibility of energy independence in America and the continuation of its position as global hegemon, while Russia and the Middle East lose out.[34]

The sorts of inequalities that exist between states at the level of natural resources and energy are obviously also bound up with the income and wealth-related inequalities between states and within them. Here, the logics are equally fraught. Income inequality in global terms is declining owing to convergence between the segments of the world economy. Inequality within states is dramatically increasing, however, as the rise of the super-rich continues.[35] For domestic statecraft, the question of national income might also resemble a sort of energy flow within the wider economy, but it clearly matters to territorial politics.[36] More pointedly, so does wealth and real estate, for they entrench inequalities that skew politics over time. Back when Kuznets was developing his approach to explaining income inequality and economic growth, he thought it was pretty clear that democracy and economic growth fostered greater migration, particularly from the country to the city. He also thought that this would eventually lead to greater wealth concentration in ever smaller population segments, bound up with entrepreneurship, technical change and the rise of a service sector.[37] Kuznets made several conjectures about these relationships at the same time as he noted various forms of protectionist legislation undertaken by the advanced democracies.[38] His data seemed to show that 'decolonization' had not yet had marked effects (unlike recent histories of the Anthropocene, which find it pivotal), but the broad contours of what has become known as the Kuznets curve were quickly elaborated. It has a familiar bell-shaped distribution, indicating a threshold moment, or a tipping point, to show that, first, market development fosters inequality, then, as development beds down, inequality decreases. The implication of Kuznets' early work, which is the important point for my purposes, is that although he thought better data were required to confirm or invalidate the hypotheses, his was a straightforward rejection of Marxist 'catastrophist' readings of modernity, where crisis is the catalyst of meaningful change. He pushed instead for the promotion of a new form of 'political and social economy' (though in fact it was actually quite old, dating back to earlier twentieth century German-speaking writers like Weber and Joseph Schumpeter).[39] That sort of social and political economy was precisely the sort of vision that Jevons had operationalized in more technical language. But Kuznets' interests have been taken up in two ways that relate to the political theory of the Anthropocene.

First, Thomas Piketty's massive book *Capital in the Twenty-First Century* radically upscales Kuznets' data sets to show widening income inequality on the premise that the rate of return to capital routinely increases more rapidly than economic growth ($r > g$). Moreover, it shows that rampant inequalities have in fact tended to be resolved or restructured only through catastrophe (war, revolution, crisis) or the political resolution and reconstruction that follows them. Now, we find ourselves in a new Belle Époque, surrounded by super-managers, hedge fund billionaires and oligarchs. But with global population changes, we find tendencies towards convergence across the globe, while the distinctions between the wealth of the wealthiest income earners and the rest, and particularly divisions within the 1%, seem to be where the action is for Piketty in terms of thinking about the site and scope of distributive justice.[40]

Secondly, however, inequality in a broader context has a much longer and more political history. In Walter Scheidel's recent retelling, human inequality developed alongside the Holocene and the domestication of food production. States emerged as the most successful of competitive institutions that could maintain stable hierarchies, and the massive inequalities they permit have tended only to be challenged fundamentally during and after wars or revolutions, or following widespread violence or disease. That these are the great levelling features of human history bodes ill for the thought that systems of economic inequality can be repurposed politically to deal with a challenge of planetary proportions like the Anthropocene. But as Scheidel also suggests, although the world is hardly a safe and steady place for large swathes of its population, the dismal levellers of old seem to have been increasingly dormant during the Great Acceleration across large parts of the world. This prompts the thought that they might eventually be overturned by modern democratic political success and stability, an unintended consequence of a system that itself relies upon minimal participation and the competitive circulation of elites.[41] The history of capitalism and economic inequality as related by Piketty and others, however, gives pause to that thought.

Wealth and income, though, are only two markers of inequality, admittedly related to more conventional socio-logical explanatory categories of race, gender and class. There are, in the language of environmentalism, both 'co-benefits' as well as shared costs that stem from trying to mobilize change in one area that affects others, and this is just as true for thinking about the Anthropocene across the sorts of axes this book has been considering. Indeed, in the wake of the dramatic weather events of recent years, another instance of the variant sources of inequality has emerged for consid-eration, namely heat inequality, particularly among those who live in cities. Because of this, many think that inter- and intra-city cooperation is much more likely to provide viable and workable local solutions to such inequalities, rather than statism or internationalism. We see instances of this all around the world, and it is certainly more straightforward to imagine cooperation between, say, Barcelona and New York than Spain and America when it comes to dealing with sustain-ability issues in global cityscapes. This will not necessarily equalize access to resources in such cities, which are often designed as much to keep poverty and homelessness hidden from the gaze of residents and tourists.[42] Global cities do, however, constitute an interesting space through which urban politics might be more radically democratized than inter-state relationships, but which also entrench new divisions between the global North and South. This is partly a result of, and partly a reaction to, a wider sort of 'urban cosmopolitan realpolitik'.[43] It is also because they rely on their own internal hierarchies and flows of power.[44] Equally, it's because the extremes of major weather events routinely hit coastal cities and low-lying areas, and as such are hyper-visible illustra-tions of the power of 'natural' disasters.[45] But somewhere between the catastrophism behind the idea of a world with less or more mitigated inequality at different points in time, and the variously optimistic or pessimistic forms of fatalism of those who say there is a cornucopia of natural resources or an inevitable solution to be found through markets and technology, lies the potential for political change through the institutional sites we already possess. Using Ulrich Beck's terms, this is the always-open space of political 'metamorphosis', the space for political choice.[46] But that space is always constrained.

In Peter H. Lindert and Jeffrey G. Williamson's book *Unequal Gains: American Growth and Inequality since 1700*, we can perhaps see why. Piketty's claim about the reconfiguration after the two world wars is repurposed as part of the 'great levelling' between c.1910 and 1970, the period of Kuznets' investigations with which this chapter began. Inequality 'plummeted' and incomes rose, as the top 1% of family income grew by 21.5%. Average US family income grew by 180%. Nearly all industrialized countries shared in this levelling. Yet three income-levelling effects were delayed in the United States until after the 1940s.[47] First, gender equality had a delayed impact, as did racial income equality, and (relatedly) the delayed rebirth of the power of the South. As Lindert and Williamson argue, Piketty doesn't explain inequality movements in the bottom 90%, which must be seen in terms of New Deal fiscal policy, slowdowns in labour supply growth (immigration was dramatically capped after the First World War) and the depression of exports.[48] After the 1970s, this changed again, which seems to suggest that we're on the up-side of another cycle of Kuznets' curves with a faster growth of labour supply, slower growth in educational attainment, shifting politics to the right, accelerated technological advances, global uncertainties and the deregulation of financial activity after periods of high tax and high regulation.[49] Given the massive diversity of the United States, this is clearly not a story with a simple pattern. But it does set up the second side of an argument about how ecological inequalities relate to Anthropocene time amid the Great Acceleration, and the idea that there are, and perhaps that there should be, limits to economic growth.

3
Limiting Growth?

The Great Acceleration forms one of the major framing perspectives on the emergence of the Anthropocene. It is part of what Dipesh Chakrabarty has referred to as a 'metabolic rift' in the three-fold classification of historical work concerning the 'earth system'; the evolution of 'human life' within that system and its limits; and the development of 'industrial civilization' or modern capitalism.[1] Put in these contexts, the Great Acceleration itself *is* part of the double movement that obviously flows alongside modern waves of decolonization and the outcomes of struggles and revolutions for national independence, and this gives us one clue as to the way in which the Anthropocene challenges conventional histories of human agency and the environment as somehow separate. It challenges the terms of such engagements themselves.

Chakrabarty's already pioneering analysis of the conjoined histories of 'climate' and 'capital' is very useful in destabilizing those oppositions. He shows the effects of the Anthropocene are pre-inscribed into the starting points you choose. How far back do we trace the origins of climate change? If we see it as human beings literally transforming their environment in ways not seen before, then it's the Anthropocene, with anthropogenic climate change as the driver. Those changes, though, are subject to both human time and geological time:

carbon dioxide in the atmosphere will dissipate eventually, and new fossil fuels will form, but human beings most likely will not live to witness this. The carbon cycle of the earth might rectify the imbalances of human production, but in its own time, and certainly not along a conventionally human time-frame. How politics and geology, or political ecology, might then produce new forms of political 'reason' differs according to your starting point. The gap that Chakrabarty talks about between cognition and action lies in the various interstices between these starting points, and those interstices have different epistemic fault lines.

Because of the dissonance between those 'natural' and 'human' time-frames, and the fact that human time horizons are bound together with the historical development of a particular set of assumptions about growth (indeed, for most mainstream economists, growth in perpetuity is a standard baseline for their models) the connections are even more complex than might be first thought. We simply cannot have a singular 'theory' of climate change that works with our sense of what politics is, or even what it might normatively require, and in any case, we do not have (nor, I would say, can we have) a singular 'theory' of politics that could incorporate anthropogenic climate change routinely into its own sense of self.

Climate change, together with its implications into various possible futures, mixes some aspects of calculable risk for human beings with a deep degree of uncertainty about outcomes, given the complexities of those feedback loops and network effects that anthropogenic climate change both presumes and affects. This, in fact, also makes thinking about energy policy within and between states so palpably complex, because there is no 'explicit characterization of uncertainty' that everyone agrees upon.[2] Moreover, because the wider ecology of the Anthropocene is relational in ways we often simply cannot understand, just like the feedback loops involved in climate change between past, present and future, it connects politics to a simultaneously deep and shallow sense of our human past. Perhaps, then, it is not so surprising that the most promising discussion of the Anthropocene as part of a modern history of the species, circulating and changing the world individually, collectively and planetarily with overlapping chronologies and temporalities, has been that which ties anthropogenic climate change to the history of capitalism with its network of flows, circulations, and representations.

Here, Marx's celebrated iconology of the capitalist world-picture as one in which the annihilation of space and time is conducted by a relational form (capital) which seeks to remake the world in its own image remains particularly apt. 'All that is solid melts into air.' But the metaphor has still further resonance for the Anthropocene. It is often forgotten that Marx's own metaphor was entirely directed to the crucial first mover of the first Anthropocene time moment, the steam engine and its role in disrupting the identity of modern subjects and selves. The actual picture painted by the phrase is of traditional solidities like class, estate, order and ideology evaporating (*verdampft*) into thin air just like steam, remaining present and changing things, but invisible to the eye. Chakrabarty's challenge is to say that Marx's focus on capital and circulation is insufficient to guide us towards an understanding of the conjoined histories of capital and climate change today. We need a different sort of political thinking with the Anthropocene front and centre, where science and politics might finally meet on equal terms, because both are geared up for critical confrontations with their past and present.[3]

However, climate science routinely digs for data in order to try to make predictions, whether in complex moral-technical analyses of what economic discount rates should be used to convert future costs and benefits into present values, or how to stabilize the uncertainty that incomplete information implies. It aims to offer versions of 'known knowns', namely how much warming is happening, how much carbon dioxide is in the atmosphere, and so forth, and then suggest solutions for human beings to try to agree upon, which of course they do not. In so doing, however, hard sciences appeal rhetorically to a vision of the earth and its planetary systems as organic, a living, vital thing, something both independent of and simultaneously dependent upon human agency. Then, of course, comes the question of interpretation. As scientists claim one thing, the historians claim another, politicians another still, and what we are left with is a series of multiple, overlapping narratives and genealogies, not all of which can easily coexist.

Consider again the different responses to the most recent IPCC report. If scientific claims about the necessity of action given limits and solid evidence were agreed upon or taken seriously, political agency should have mobilized to act on climate change a generation ago. But we are still asking questions as to what the tipping points of the climate cycle will be; whether we can even know them in advance even if we cannot predict their exact effects; and even if we know what we either could, or should, do. For these are judgements about risk and probability that occur within indeterminate or vague thresholds, epistemic limits and even radical uncertainty. Given this, is a precautionary principle the right way to go? Act now to preserve jam today, and in so doing preserve your jam for tomorrow, might be the mantra. But the challenge to the precautionary principle under the Anthropocene is one of scale.[4] The strategies for thinking about how we preserve jam today and still get jam tomorrow are more easily redescribed by politicians in operational or catastrophic terms, which allows them to focus almost exclusively on their national terrain. Donald Trump's slogan of Making America Great Again, for example, aligns with just such a project, where American 'exceptionalism' has, rather exceptionally in modern American history, been dethroned. Here is old-style fear and loathing curated anew, in a spin on a very old resource-related problem. For example, consider Thomas Meaney's discussion of Donald Trump and the environment with Peter Sloterdijk in a recent feature for the *New Yorker*:

> When we spoke about Trump, Sloterdijk explained him as part of a shift in Western history. 'This is a moment that won't come again,' he told me. 'Both of the old Anglophone empires have within a short period withdrawn from the universal perspective.' Sloterdijk went so far as to claim that Trump uses fears of ecological devastation in his favor. 'The moment for me was when I first heard him say "America First,"' he said. 'That means: America to the front of the line! But it's not the line for globalization anymore, but the line for resources. Trump channels this global feeling of ecological doom.'[5]

*

How should we understand this linkage of resources, globalization and the political mobilization of climate catastrophe under the Anthropocene across the period of the Great Acceleration?[6] One seemingly plausible route, much in vogue since the inauguration of Donald Trump and the seeming rise of numerous anti-liberal populist parties and governments, takes us back to the context of the 1930s and 1940s as a prologue to the present. Here it is easy to find the darker intellectual origins of 'America First', though perhaps it doesn't offer quite the right temporal arc within which to understand our own moment. Contemporary democracies are certainly now much older, much more entrenched, much richer, and with often very different demographic markers. Thinking of contemporary democratic collapse necessarily leading to fascist tyranny doesn't seem quite right.[7] Equally, the increased interconnection of the global economy and macro-finance since at least the early 1970s has changed the context in which politics takes place. Then, claims around a New International Economic Order challenged the moral and intellectual hegemony of the global 'North'; the 1973 OPEC crisis and IMF loans in Britain symbolized an energy regime under significant geopolitical strain; while the evolution of the European Community into a larger European Union and the general rise of what has come to be termed a regime of neoliberalism formed the parabola through which we might more readily think about the global interconnections that fix the coordinates of the Anthropocene.[8]

To the extent that the global financial crises of 2007–8 signify the proximate origins of the election of Trump and other anti-liberal populists, its roots in turn lie in the rapid slowdown in economic growth in the 1970s and the competitive outsourcing overseas of traditional jobs. Wolfgang Streeck has made the argument that the slowdown in growth in the 1970s in advanced Northern democracies did not ultimately result in a 'legitimation' crisis of capitalism, which he and several other (notably German) writers, like Jürgen Habermas and Claus Offe, had predicted.[9] Then, they worried about the loss of steering capacity by an overcommitted state, which threatened the political viability of welfare provision and environmental sustainability. Now, looking back, Streeck at least suggests this was not a true legitimation

crisis for capitalism. Such a crisis was 'delayed' by governments dealing in a short-term fashion with wider structural
problems of indebtedness and low growth. As he suggests,
borrowing analytical categories from Joseph Schumpeter,
modern American and European styles of representative
politics evolved strategies for dealing with income generation
(taxation) and indebtedness (whether personal or sovereign)
in combined forms of a 'tax state' until the end of the Great
War. There then emerged a 'debt' state after the Second
World War and into the 1970s. With the breakdown of a
so-called 'Keynesian consensus' thereafter, a modern 'consoli-
dation' state arose, with post-Fordist production methods
and an increased focus on the mixed modes of capitalist
development. These transitions had their own intellectual
markers and ideologues. In the early post-war period, new
sorts of managerial economentality in firms like Kodak and
ITT used Eastern mysticism to construe managers as global
gurus, in pursuit of a Zen-like focus on the interconnected
web of nature and environment and business or profit, but
which continued to require rapacious extraction at yet more
frontier zones of the world economy.[10] A Protestant work
ethic and modern organizational theory were new versions of
these stories, found in writings from Peter Drucker to Kenichi
Ohmae at the level of management theory, while post-
Marxist academics tried to theorize the relative autonomy of
the state in relation to capitalism.[11]

   In Streeck's rendition (which, interestingly, combines both
a critique of neoliberalism as ideology and a defence of
neo-Marxist state theory), the advanced democracies have
now moved out of the high-inflation and low-debt world of
the 1970s. After a low-inflation and high-debt period from
1980 to 1993, low inflation continued until 2007, but with
a transition from high public to high private debt. Since the
world economic system crashed in 2008, we have seen low
inflation and high debt at both public and private levels, and
public debt takes the form of a *distributional conflict between
creditors and citizens*.[12] That sort of distributional issue is
precisely where new forms of climate financing might appear,
moving forward today.[13] But what signals a major difference
from the 1970s to the present at the level of economic strategy
is how unimaginative any of the current solutions for dealing

with our situation are. In the 1970s, although one might look back wearily or with cynicism depending upon your age, the sheer variety of strategies for economic renewal, economic democracy, workers cooperatives and industrial democracy, and more, reveals a vibrant debate about possibility. Now, if it doesn't involve quantitative easing in a new era of secular stagnation and low interest rates, filtered through networks of powerful gatekeepers in central banks and international organizations, it is derided as rampant utopianism and a threat to stability. It is perhaps no surprise that in such a context, many have wondered whether or not our own age of globalization is over.[14]

What has changed, it seems, with the perspective of yet another generational time-lag, is a major transformation in the ratios of public to private debt along with massive austerity, while a hollowing out of the state at local and national levels has occurred while international organizations secured more authority and guidance. Any pretence at full employment is gone, as inflation control has become the priority of prudential statecraft in a complexly globalized and interconnected banking system that hardly anyone really understands. Taken together, these mark the coordinates of what has become shorthand for the rise of modern 'neoliberalism'. They signal for writers like Streeck, now, a failure of 'capitalism' though not of 'democracy', and the failure of a model that for a century or more has justified itself with the promise, real or illusory, of perpetual economic growth and increasing prosperity. Globalization now means the rise of inequality. Ironically, though, there are those who seek a second singularity from 'peak globalization', where proximity between production and consumption (think 3D printing, vertical farms and cultured meat production) might be the technological move that eventually forces the economy to 'put people first', rather than pursue economic growth for its own sake.[15]

*

That might sound utopian once more, but utopias as critiques of contemporary forms of sociability, and as ways of criticizing contemporary nostrums about what is natural or not, are a mainstay of green political thinking.[16] In *Social Limits to Growth*, Fred Hirsch outlined the increasingly tentacular reach of commodification and the 'commercialization effect' of modern capitalism as it reached into such apparently private spheres as love and sexuality, rendering them legible within the parameters of modern economic rationality and calculation.[17] Yet once one places these considerations within the wider contours of environmental calculation, recognizing the interconnections between space, place, goods and people, then it is possible to engage in a still-deeper critique of marketization and financialization. As Hirsch wrote, 'Orgasm as a consumer's right rather rules it out as an ethereal experience,'[18] but equally, one might add, understanding the currents of human sexuality makes sense only within the broader awareness of how human approaches to sexuality have changed across time and space.

That Michel Foucault's hugely influential series of studies on histories of sexuality were appearing around the same time seems like one further connection with Hirsch's agenda. But both relate to the thought that seems to keep returning in each generation, namely that as societies get richer, they find that affluence does not lead to happiness.[19] That seems to be an obvious result if we think that happiness requires something more than merely economic prosperity, when we know that entrenched wealth tends to systematically distort policy outcomes and political dynamics across generations.[20] What we value now must always be recognized as being historically contingent, and for those worried about the 'limits' to growth in the early 1970s, this meant then, as perhaps it still means now, that the principal problem affecting economically prosperous and advanced democracies is the 'structural need to pull back from economic self-advancement'.[21] That is to say, it is the need to see through the presumption of cornucopianism and perpetual growth that is the mythology or ideology of modern democratic capitalism, and which is now bursting at the seams as demographic transitions, low growth, economic precarity for the young and major social cleavages emerge, which are naturalized in ways that are anything but natural.[22] The sort of 'privatized Keynesianism' that once delayed the real effects of an economy in crisis seems to have come to an end.[23]

Hirsch's book was very much about Britain and America, and appeared in the wake of various issues already mentioned: an IMF loan crisis affecting the British state and the OPEC oil price rises earlier in that decade; and, shortly after, Gerald Ford's calls in 1976 for America to become energy independent by 1985.[24] His analysis also appeared five years after the influential multi-author study conducted by the Club of Rome with the title *The Limits to Growth* (1972). The result of a meeting in Rome of 1968, this report was principally technical in its focus, and geared towards understanding the exponential implications of forms of growth and particular growth regimes. It is similar to the thought that Thomas Piketty has more recently made famous, that those individuals or firms who start big and gain returns on investment are likely to grow more quickly and be more successful over the long run than not. That's because growth and profit return is exponential, not linear, so that more leads to more over time. Broadened out to consider a world threatened by 'the arms race, environmental deterioration, the population explosion and economic stagnation',[25] some sort of calculus was required to explain how these artificial human problems should be understood and then tackled. To this end, the Club of Rome mobilized a model of the world constructed and computerized at MIT, and designed it to understand these and related issues mathematically by modelling exponential rates (i.e. 'increases by a constant percentage of the whole in a constant time period'[26]) rather than linear growth rates. As they say, 'If the present growth trends in world population, industrialization, pollution, food production, and resource depletion continue unchanged, the limits to growth on this planet will be reached sometime within the next hundred years.'[27] They may yet still be right. Moreover, not only will exponential growth of those things which are necessarily limited and finite result in their eventual end (that is clear), but also the dynamic model of limits to growth here presumes both a positive and a negative feedback loop. In this, population growth has been 'super-exponential', as it continues to be.[28] And ultimately, they write, a 'decision to do nothing' about all this is still a decision, and that means that there are still options, that there is still hope. 'Deliberately limiting growth would be difficult,

but not impossible.'[29] By the time of their thirty-year update
on this, the authors were 'much more pessimistic' about that
because humanity 'is already in unsustainable territory'.[30]

In the 1970s, however, such thoughts easily aligned with
contemporaneous calls by deep ecologists to pursue much
more environmentally sustainable lifestyles, sometimes
grounded in a philosophical framework of 'ecosophy'. Other
critics developed a post-industrial sensibility to propose new
'paradigms of work' and basic income provision for a zero-
growth society. These were often rejected then as rather
wilful and potentially authoritarian cries in the wilderness by
people who didn't like technology.[31] But then, as again now,
breaking the stranglehold of established ways of thinking
about economic growth remains extraordinarily difficult,
because although there are any number of possible as
well as plausible technical considerations in the attempt to
leverage political success out of the idea of an economically
'stationary' state, they have to do with wider issues of how
we might understand the relationship between change and
progress, particularly how the one might not be connected
to the other. Biologists like Paul Ehrlich were, at the time,
beginning to make this issue into a new commonplace.[32]

The evidence of sweeping population shifts, environmental
calamities and war in the later 1960s suggested straightforwardly for Ehrlich at least that there was nothing naturally
'balanced' or in equilibrium about nature, a theme taken up
by eco-democrats ever since.[33] Biological theories which
presupposed balance, much like earlier political theories
assuming the same, were clearly out of date.[34] Correlatively,
the idea that there were straightforwardly 'natural' limits to
growth was satirized and castigated in its own time, even
though it was part of a wider scene in which numerous other
neo-Malthusian books and articles were being published.
Perhaps the most famous other instance here was Jay W.
Forrester's *World Dynamics*, which was savaged by critics
(as was the wider *Limits to Growth* analysis by the Club
of Rome) as merely 'Malthus with a Computer'. In a major
response that criticized the simplicity of the modelling in
both analyses, opponents challenged the presumption that
future changes would of necessity be like past ones, and
accused its authors of neglecting even the possibility of

alternative improvements.[35] Moreover, despite pessimism about these models, economists like Robert Solow suggested at the time that population was hardly a problem at all, in fact. Using different economic models that assumed that there was always some 'optimum' somewhere to be found meant that there were no 'difficult conceptual problems' about population in the context of resource constraints at least at the level of theory. The end of the world was very clearly not just around the corner for everyone.[36]

Thinking of the limits to growth often presupposes the possibility of the transformation of values surrounding growth, or at the very least a re-evaluation of seemingly natural economic values. That also seems to require a rejection of something akin to the dominant ideology of modern capitalism, namely the presumption of a cornucopia of resources that will fuel unstoppable growth as the natural order of things. For some, the virtue of returning to the idea that there are 'limits to growth' now is that capitalism has itself reached a new evolutionary stage, a 'cancer stage', where 'growth for growth's sake' has become unnatural, a sickness that needs to be treated by promoting a new approach to human well-being. This would be one that goes well beyond what we already know and that such measures as GDP cannot very well capture.[37] Well-being in this new order would require resilience, forms of eco-security and a sense that human flourishing will need new ways of dealing with old problems. 'Frugality' would need to become a new sort of 'generosity', and useful 'labour' would be preferred to 'useless toil', an obvious updating of an old romantic socialist trope. All of this requires a sort of 'non-wasteful efficiency' with energy, and even 'green growth'.[38]

We have seen already that the composite times of the Anthropocene reflect the transitions of dominant energy regimes, from steam and coal to oil, towards nuclear, wind and solar power, among others. These transitions come with their own forms of reasoning and justification, their own sort of epistemic 'economentalities'. For Timothy Mitchell, the origins of a modern 'economentality' lies in the later 1940s, emerging alongside the development of oil pipelines and new measurement techniques, out of the slump in fuel availability in America during the winter of 1947–8.[39] The liquid flow of this crude energy found an easy fit with models of economic forecasting based on resource flows and trends, a constantly shifting signal of profit and loss on the screen, global and impersonal in reach but also still nationally driven. In ways that other new histories are beginning to show, this moment of nationally driven responses to global dilemmas through new economic frames of reference was mirrored by the welfarist strategies used to entrench the otherwise universal moral demands of the Universal Declaration of Human Rights.[40] This makes the emergence of modern economentality in the age of human rights part of an accelerated Anthropocene time. Nonetheless, the idea of perpetual economic growth based on the extraction and use of an in principle limitless energy is a well-established trope in the history of economic discourse, stretching from Francis Bacon in the early seventeenth century to David Ricardo in the early nineteenth century, well before it reached the 'growthman' economists around Solow at MIT in the 1950s.[41] Such fluctuating oppositions between different styles of fatalism about resources and political possibilities, whether optimistic or pessimistic, have become something of a repeating pattern in the evolution of modern representative politics and its energy regimes.[42]

*

On the other side of this debate, however, are those who think not only that we might need to consider growth and energy in terms of their relationship to political values and choices, but also that human beings might be best served by seeking solace in a low-growth or 'stationary state' economy. What does that mean? Well, the idea of the 'stationary state' has a long and interesting intellectual history. One early interpreter in the middle of the eighteenth century was Adam Smith, and his sense of the place of the stationary state as a rather dull, but certainly rather to be expected (though temporary) end to equally temporary eras of progress or decline. His understanding of there being some sort of 'natural' balance to the economy, as was suggested by those who referred to the population–resource balance required in the Scottish Highlands, for example, was that this had in fact been knocked off-kilter generations ago.[43] As the idea developed, however, one of its principal supporters in the mid-nineteenth century was John Stuart Mill, who implied that once growth had succeeded in satisfying basic human needs, a stationary state model could allow for the pursuit of higher pleasures.

Mill's interpretation, one perhaps more famously emblematized by John Maynard Keynes in the later 1920s, was that once basic needs of subsistence and production were met, the 'economy' could become stationary in the sense of being motivated less by 'profit' and more according to a different socio-cultural metric. This was a plan in praise of 'idleness', in the Bloomsbury iteration of Bertrand Russell, or the 'bliss' state of Frank Ramsey, another of Keynes's colleagues. In practical terms, modern automation, increased efficiencies and the provision of minimum living standards would mean less time would need to be devoted to physical 'labour', leaving more time for the so-called 'higher' pursuits and leisure. The stationary state, on this account, is, to some degree, a practical attempt to call a halt to unfettered capitalism without ushering in any kind of socialist or communist future, a search for a putative third way that has continued to structure debate at least since Mill. The question of whether a 'stationary' state requires, or indeed aims at, restoring something like 'balance' similarly remained a central question for the 'no-growth' or 'limits to growth' agenda in the 1960s and 1970s. Balance, though, was often redescribed to mean whatever kind of 'viable economic environment' might make possible a stable population through time without a decline in quality of life. After all, if there is no natural 'balance' to nature, creating a viable economic environment might better be redescribed as the search for stability. That is, ecological balance 'hinges' on its effect upon human consumption levels, such that if fossil fuels were used up before new techniques in fusion made nuclear power or alternative energy sources viable, then this would lead to a situation of ecological 'imbalance'. Stationary states cannot achieve ecological balance on this model, but they might go beyond contemporary debates about growth.[44]

The stationary state idea often reappears whenever there is a decline or slowdown in economic 'growth'. In historical work on the subject, for example, one finds much recent discussion of Japan in the 1980s as a state whose growth had basically flatlined, but which has continued to be a low-growth but prosperous and stable economy. Similarly, one can find discussion of the same problem and place in the mid-1890s, just prior to the rapid rise of Japanese imperial power. Kenneth Boulding, one of the pioneering ecological economists associated with the population debates at the end of the 1960s and the beginning of the 1970s, wrote shortly after the release of the Club of Rome report that with the addition of pollution to the Malthusian devils of overpopulation and diminishing resources, the metaphor of 'spaceship earth' would soon enough have to become a reality. What was needed was a sense of 'economy in which all materials must be recycled and in which ultimately the sun is the only source of energy'.[45] It brings to mind the image on the front cover of this book – where the earth seems to be melting amid the heat of the sun on the dial that measures its time, time that is running out.

That might be a rather apocalyptic image against which to set politics. But the early instance of a sundial, a human curation of a time regime built to understand the relationship between the revolutions of the Earth and other planets and stars in a still wider system, shows how human beings have long thought of their own place in a universe that they are not wholly in control of, but which sets their lifespans in contexts that are more than merely economic or growth-related. Of course, the extreme development of a relationship between time as the twenty-four-hour clock, with work-discipline and modern capitalism across a global vista, has long been known.[46] But such work-time has always engendered a form of radical-ethical criticism too, central to historical traditions of political economy, though often submerged today under something like the 'philanthrocapitalism' associated with the extremely wealthy.[47]

If earlier moral critics of capitalism had long recognized the arbitrary but hugely powerful quality of using time to discipline labour, ecological economists like Boulding expanded this terrain. Boulding wanted to consider both territorial and non-territorial dimensions of the biosphere as the global system within which human energy and activity takes place.

He used the illustration of territorial responses to conventional Malthusian limits by looking at the strategies adopted by individual members of particular species, comparing the robin or house cat, for example, and contrasting them with the wider group-led responses of, say, alley cats. Finding an individual territory away from others of your species, one that can be forcefully defended (with some help from other living creatures, particularly humans), offers a good survival strategy because it recognizes the need for living within your limits. Group responses, on this account, seem to trigger worse outcomes for individuals in terms of food and survival. For while you rarely see scrawny house cats or robins, the cartoon image of the undernourished alley cat is closer to the mark. So it looks like the best outcome of a stationary state when applied to human beings is to limit places given finite resources, rather than have to deal with a struggle for survival prompted by a declining food supply. However, the stationary state might be a more likely possibility once certain sorts of generational inequalities have been locked in, so to speak, and there's less chance of the rich getting poorer, or the poor getting richer – so even though one group prevails over another, there is 'no escape from the rigors of scarcity'.[48]

Moderate scarcity, though, has formed the background assumption of most historically sensitive modern political theory towards economic distribution. From eighteenth-century figures like Smith and Hume, a sense of natural human and economic inequality mixed with an equally natural capacity for propriety, emulation and resentment prompted an artificial and conjectural narrative about the evolution of institutions of justice and government. From here, a theory of the state emerged that was premised on an understanding of a limited but foundational human sociability, mixing commercial forms of reciprocity with a sort of natural deference to conventional authority.[49] This sort of commercial sociability, for shorthand, works quite well with the idea of a development towards the stationary state.

In fact, for political theorists, it is quite interesting that John Rawls saw the possibilities of a stationary state as one plausible end point to his vision of a just society, one that had evolved a basic structure of constitutional fairness from the premises of moderate scarcity and regulated inequality, and had at least a 'purely procedural' analysis of what justice requires in terms of improving conditions for the worst off. Entrenching an efficient regime of 'property-owning democracy' over time between close or proximate generations (his was a limited model of inter-generational justice) by producing and utilizing a 'just savings rate', this model of democratic and technocratic or efficiency-driven politics would be compatible with a stationary state (perhaps even forms of universal basic income).[50] It requires continuous attention to allocation, distribution, stabilization and transfers between its population (and it could be a model for relations between different peoples), but without the conventional requirements of economic growth. Moreover, because 'peoples' for Rawls are analogous to 'states', artificial entities that exhibit shared characteristics – cultures and institutional memories and histories, for example – the stationary state of the just society offers one possible vision of liberal democracy stabilizing into the distant future by continuously responding to its present. Such an efficiency-driven model of a property-owning democracy developed after a long and complex engagement with yet another British economist, James Meade.[51]

Rawls's sense of securing justice for proximate generations resonated with the interest of contemporary welfare economists like Meade, Robert Solow, Amartya Sen and others, and meant in his case (in contrast to some wilful discussion in modern political theory) a deep engagement with the real politics of property ownership, taxation rates and how to stabilize 'fair' institutions.[52] His sense of the wider psychology behind the 'sense of justice' people have, and which might motivate them, was also much broader than conventional economic models. It bound together themes from Rousseau and Smith about moral sentiments, and incorporated claims from Kant and Hegel about unsocial sociability, the ideal of the state as a form of ethical life, and the legitimation of rational action at the bar of publicly justifiable reasons. Furthermore, using Jean Piaget's work, he developed a claim about human psychology and development through childhood, of flourishing and love, which for Rawls was exemplified by the nurturing of children in the nuclear family. That rather conservative note clearly aligned with the male-breadwinner model that first underpinned many welfare state regimes, and occluded the politics of the private sphere, as feminist critics quickly noted. Rawls's mid-century American Protestant worldview nonetheless compelled him also to think about the natural goodness of persons as distinct and discrete selves (something he thought utilitarianism neglected), but in principle perfectible through the right institutions and distributional regimes, where social life becomes akin to a form of secular theodicy.[53] Within all this, Rawls seems to have been thinking about the relationship between economic growth and the future stability of a just polity, in ways that look more in line with an holistic and ecological, rather than mainstream, form of economics.[54]

In fact, in the same year that Rawls's *Theory of Justice* appeared and with the same publisher, Nicholas Georgescu-Roegen's seminal text for ecological economics, *The Entropy Law and the Economic Process*, was published.[55] That book, by a student of Schumpeter, focused on the idea of the eventual depletion of energy to an entropic state, and was in turn hugely influential on the work of one of his students, perhaps the leading analyst of the idea of the stationary state, Herman Daly. Outside of ecological economics, the book has been rather forgotten in the wake of Rawls's influence, but in Daly's early elaboration, the entropy result from Georgescu-Roegen dovetailed with an analysis of criss-crossing feedback loops involved in understanding holistic ecological perspectives on economics. Georgescu-Roegen remained pessimistic, seeing entropy all the way down that even the 'stationary' state could not offset, for no state can live forever in a 'finite' environment.[56] Daly's views, however, were initially combined with his reading of Rachel Carson's *Silent Spring* as well as an understanding of uneven global development, given personal research he had done in some of the poorest areas of Brazil. Combined and uneven development leading towards a stationary state was part and parcel of his wider ecological rendering of what he termed the economic subsystem.

The technicalities of an entropic economy versus the stationary state are recounted by Daly in a recent interview, but he still retains a focus on the 'stationary' or 'steady-state' economy. The economy remains a subsystem of the 'larger system, the ecosphere, which is finite, non-expanding, materially closed. It is open to a flow of solar energy, but the Sun itself is non-growing.' If the 'subsystem keeps growing', he argues, 'it eventually coincides with the whole parent system, at which point it'll have to behave as a steady state'. Not a state devoid of development and change, but one that recognizes the limits imposed by scale and size. Seeing things in this way allows him to distinguish practically between the quantitative states of 'growth' and more qualitative measures of 'development', and that focus on the qualitative rather than the quantitative is where Daly proposes political economy in Anthropocene time needs to engage. It is here that politics can be salvaged amid technical, geo-economic debates about energy, growth resources and limits.[57]

In political terms, thinking about the steady state implies the need to recognize that massive inequalities of wealth and income are dramatically disruptive, such that maximum as well as minimum income levels will likely form part of a package of policies that could offset the delusions of perpetual, unfettered growth. Talking about limiting population might also be required, though this is clearly a fraught discourse. Writers like Boulding, for example, were so inspired by Mill they thought that one might do for population what Mill had suggested for voting. Mill, himself a strong paternalist when it came to the duty of governments to limit population growth, particularly among those communities of people who lacked resources to provide for their offspring, nevertheless thought that all should in principle have a vote.[58] However, Mill thought that some, perhaps predictably the more educated, should have more than one vote. Boulding offered the idea, 'a little tongue in cheek', of 'marketable licenses for having babies', which of course sounds offensive to many. His wider point, though, was that one might conceive of a situation in which levels of inequality had reduced to such an extent that new arrangements might not merely replicate the further advantages of the already rich and powerful. Moreover, a broad 'systems consciousness' in the contemporary moment about the need for holistic social science might make people see the point of addressing population questions prospectively, before the 'utterly dismal theorem' of eventual overpopulation and starvation could kick in.[59] The intellectual point was to try to see what insight a focus on energy (input–throughput–output) models might offer when considering the political economy of the stationary state as it moves into the future beyond the constitutional 'form' of liberalism and the ethical 'substance' of socialism.[60] And just as energy physics revolutionized economic theory in the nineteenth century, some energy-based ecological economics offer radical alternatives to the conventional growth models of modern capitalism, some of which were particularly pertinent to the moment of 'post-industrialism' in the post-war period.[61]

This has recently returned to political salience in post-capitalist thinking, through figures like Paul Mason on the social-democratic left and Nick Land on an accelerationist-libertarian trajectory, as well as in general histories of the end of humanity in the post-humanist future of artificial intelligence and robots as envisaged by Yuval Harari.[62] Earlier writers like André Gorz and others who sought new utopias in the post-industrial landscape of a previous generation looked towards what one sympathetic critic, Boris Fraenkel, called 'eco-socialist semi-autarky' from the later 1970s and into the 1980s. Here, rather than a sort of liberal defence of individual privacy against market intrusion, socialist reason was redefined to show that it, too, valued individual projects and individual desires, which were the essence of what a collective political socialism might ground itself upon in a post-industrial era of a planned or steady-state economy.[63] This is analogous to the debate between market socialists and socialist critics of the market in recent Marxism, which has simultaneously become a set of reflections about how to 'green' Marxism and make it more than merely a political theory of 'survival' in the face of seemingly impossible liberation.[64] Yet those who think markets can be tempered and that capitalists can be persuaded to limit growth stand on one side, opposed on the other by those who think that, structurally, markets and capitalism cannot exist without seeking perpetual growth and profit.[65]

Radical eco-socialists think differently still, often rejecting the idea of a steady-state economy, either because of a de-growth agenda, or owing to the focus on population management in steady-state models.[66] Instead, they focus on territory, and might do so now, in particular, with reference to land scarcity. Here, the claim is that 'natural' rather than 'artificial' geo-engineering, by repurposing extant lands and pastures, is the best plan to reduce carbon and slow growth, and also aligns with the hopeful avoidance of a 'sixth extinction'. To do this requires a massive amount of free land, however, and this is in short supply.[67] Indeed, a version of re-wilding the planet would require the decommissioning of nuclear power, a move to electric and renewables (quickly adapted to thanks to technological innovations), a rapid shift towards vegetarianism and a transformation of the agribusiness sector. More recent proposals, such as that proposed by E. O. Wilson, among others, offer new versions of those narratives that rely on better environmental data, and which change patterns of global land use in ways that don't seem to directly threaten individual consumption like older ecological criticisms of unsustainable consumption were wont to do.[68] Yet although this sort of 'global Cuba' strategy might be a rational solution to an irrational international system, its environmental politics still sounds rather austere. In fact, from the perspective of the history of political thought, this is but one more version of the 'closed commercial state' model from Fichte and Rousseau onwards, rethought for Anthropocene time.[69] It might sound as utopian now to globalize autarky as a rational strategy for dealing with the 'commons' of the earth as Fichte's and Rousseau's plans to step off the evolutionary treadmill of modern commercial society seemed to many of their critics. What unites both eras is that such utopianism is based upon a realistic critique about where we are. If we see ecological catastrophe everywhere and find its roots in a system of capitalism, just as eighteenth-century critics saw a negative relationship between economic competition and human progress in an age of commercial globalization, then rather than counselling despair, we might perhaps target our anger towards those whose actions need to change most radically.[70]

This can, of course, take numerous, paradoxical forms. Libertarians who claim to see the writing on the wall might go off-grid, buying up land in remote areas of New Zealand (or, possibly, stepping off the planet altogether) to engage in individualistic forms of survivalism. Internationalists might try to target firms and financial elites, whether through strategies of divestment or forms of direct action, to shift the terms of engagement. Whether or not we reject despair and harness utopian promise, however, we are also bound to think about whether the sorts of trends in energy policy and international geopolitics that we see today could offer more straightforward hope for an environmentally sustainable future. The pragmatic geo-energy vision of someone like Dieter Helm, for example, does suggest some interesting recent developments in this direction.

In the blunter terms pursued in his forthright assessment *The Carbon Crunch*, 'Anyone deluding themselves that we will be *forced* to decarbonize because we don't have enough fossil fuels needs to look at the facts.' Furthermore, this 'isn't going to happen in the relevant timescale for tackling global warming – if ever'.[71] Yet now he thinks that the resource-rich and early-oil-adapting USA will, in the context of its natural resources and space, its capacity to capitalize on the interim power of gas, and its combination of technological innovation and democratic adaptivity, retain its global hegemony and realize its 1970s dream of energy independence. As the continuous evolution of fossil fuel and carbon-based extractive energy politics shows, shale-fracking options have indeed, a generation after Jimmy Carter, made energy independence at the hemispheric level of the northern United States into a real possibility. Relatedly, as Paul Krugman suggests, a basic strategy that pursues mitigation needs the USA to move first, given its per capita lead in carbon emissions.[72] So, the USA might lead the way into the Anthropocened politics of the future through a sort of energy-autarky model for others to follow or engage with – an ironic-sounding possibility, given President Trump's at least rhetorical commitment to isolationism. At the same time, though, resource-rich but less adaptable or less networked and diversified economies, such as Saudia Arabia or Russia, will, in the end, weaken, according to Helm. This would bode well for Europe, too.[73]

Yet it is important to remember that most other states in the global economy with the regional capacity to actually move to low-carbon economies are those who are marginalized within its structures, and historically poor.[74] This in turn suggests that regional cooperation is most possible where it is least immediately consequential, mirroring some of the claims made by powerful states like China and India about Western-driven demands for global cooperation. It also suggests that international cooperation from within (at city or regional level) and between states who see themselves as part of a global commons might be able to trigger new patterns of investment that could meet the sorts of challenges laid out in *The Carbon Crunch*, and updated in *Natural Capital: Valuing the Planet*.[75] In that book, Helm also advances the idea of legislating ecological demands into the tax code in order to compel compliance towards the need to meet certain sorts of carbon emission targets. But he remains adamant that carbon avoidance and the turn to renewables alone as salvation is nothing more than a fool's errand. As there is more than enough carbon to be used for generations, to be truly motivational and action guiding, climate change needs to be tackled by taxation and economic pricing in the normal way.

For even if there is hope that coordinated environmental policy within Europe, or energy independence in America, for example, might point towards wider global change under the superintendence of international organizations, laws and norms, few politicians will ever come straight out and say 'climate change is all about coal, economic growth and population growth'.[76] Making them do so will require honesty about the pain to follow, but the challenge of the Anthropocene might provide the impetus here. Why? Because the language through which pleas for action upon climate change and energy consumption are delivered seem often to be modelled on the idea of a war to save the planet. Indeed, Helm's analogy between peacetime and wartime economics works well at this level of debate, highlighting that the realities required to offset climate change will require dramatic changes to consumption levels in order to provide room for new sorts of environmentally sensitive production. But the analogy is self-defeating in another way. For when politicians re-prioritize the national, seeking comparative advantage from international trade and domestic benefits from secure national resources, then the politics of climate change, even if it transitions to energy regimes more quickly than Helm once thought, might just result in new forms of trade wars over similarly scarce resources, with no real political change at all.

All told, there might be little more to this future than the sort of 'sorry comfort' once offered by international lawyers and political theorists who justified European dominance over colonial territories with reference to arbitrary standards of 'civilization'.[77] Anthropocened politics cannot follow such a route alone, because the still more potent challenge it presents is in how to retrospectively understand, account for and perhaps rectify past injustices by acknowledging the inequalities and debts owed in the present to those who were previously and unjustly exploited, expropriated and extinguished. One of the more interesting issues raised in this constellation of thinking about indebtedness in Anthropocene time, particularly of the global North to the global South, has been to think about what is entailed in reconstituting these debts as 'ecological'.

4

Ecological Debts

Historians of political and economic thought have long been accustomed to dealing with the central conundrums of credit and debt in the emergence of modern states. As European states expanded in the eighteenth century, the emergence of what has been called the 'fiscal-military' state emerged very clearly in England, France and Spain as part of the wider evolution of a new wave of capitalist development.[1] The French revolutionary crisis was, after all, at least in part dependent upon a massive sovereign debt crisis, which required the King to call the Estates General to assemble for the first time in over a century, and to try to authorize tax rises to pay for the increasing costs of credit being used to finance expansionist wars. Many of the most important modern writers on politics quickly saw the dangers of what Hume called the 'rhapsody' of public debt, a potentially endless cycle of debt financing in the service of continued belligerence. Here, credit itself posed a direct challenge to the prominent idea that commercial interaction and the development of capitalism would, through profit and trade, lead to a softening of national jealousies and secure a more lasting peace.[2]

In our own time, such distributional dilemmas have been rehearsed in debates about 'democratic peace' and globalization. Dani Rodrik has christened as a paradox of this system the fact that economic growth, representative democracy and peace cannot naturally coexist with one another at all times and in all places.[3] Ever since the First World War, in fact, where the implications of the end of another period of 'great moderation' were temporarily stabilized by 'functional internationalism' acting as a sort of ideological glue, logics of economic convergence as much as divergence have been the norm. That is one of the analogous structural connections between the Great War and the Great Recession, as one historian of both, Adam Tooze, has wryly noted.[4] Of course, the added complexity of the global financial system and inter-bank lending today overlays a sort of macro-financial regime even more difficult to fathom than that which operated during the First World War. In the early twentieth century, however, as today, the system was governed by networks of agencies and actors that often shared something in common sociologically, and perhaps only because they did, were they able to work together to contain potentially global meltdowns.

Nevertheless, in the wake of the First World War, some figures who have retained their importance in debates about environmental or ecological economics, particularly the old Cambridge economics don Arthur Pigou (whose tax on negative externalities remains the polestar of the 'polluter pays' principle), talked about the need for a special levy on capital to cover the costs of wartime reparations and debt payments. Other forms of inter-generational taxation would disproportionately affect the poorest in society, Pigou thought, so instead he worked to justify a more progressive solution that would do right by the poor in both the present the future.[5] And if the Anthropocene is war by other means, the lessons of wartime finance debates might be worth reconsidering for contemporary politics. Indeed, it is no surprise that the sort of massive capital levies on profitable firms and those who had done well financially out of wartime which were proposed by Pigou among others are once again being taken up by contemporary economists. In a very recent manifesto piece, Thomas Piketty has called for a similar 'squeeze' on the rich across Europe, funding research and action on climate change and inequality by four major taxes, understood as the 'tangible markers' of a 'European solidarity', in the hope of fostering a step-change in our own politics.[6]

These, as well as other puzzles of sovereign debt and private debt, credit-rating scores and lending capacity, are also fairly standard fare in contemporary discussions of political thought and environmental justice. And when economic growth rates tend to decline, as they have in the West since the 1970s, it is possible to question once again whether or not the expectation of perpetual prosperity under capitalist democracy remains more than a useful myth. In such a context, and in the generational perspective offered since the financial crash of 2008, it is hardly surprising that the theory and practice of sovereign indebtedness have returned to the agenda with new force, and that generational perspectives have sought to find the origins of this system that permitted levels of state as well as personal credit and debt to balloon in historically unprecedented orders of magnitude. For critics like Streeck, as we have seen, the chief culprit is a dominant ideology of neoliberalism, newly resurgent in the 1970s with the decline of the post-war Keynesian welfare state in Europe and Anglo-America and the end of Bretton Woods. It lies behind a series of policy options that merely staved off another sort of legitimation crisis facing modern capitalism, whose fruits were forty years of widening inequality of wealth and property, and an inevitable reckoning that 2008 provided.[7]

In turn, what these perspectives combining political economy and political theory often neglect are the connections to a wider political ecology of capitalism based around profiteering and debt financing in the still longer term. Those interested in the growth-driven dynamics of capitalism and nature and newly attuned to the concept of the Anthropocene have tried to begin to think about the various ways in which the globally combined and uneven nature of capitalist development allows us to see the concept of debt and indebtedness in new ways. Analogous counter-concepts to the novelty of the Anthropocene, such as the 'Capitalocene', have been developed by writers like Jason Moore to illustrate these conjoined histories of capitalism and ecological exploitation.[8] Together with Raj Patel, Moore offers an alternative balance sheet where debts owed by the early winners of modern capitalism could, and should, be repaid to the losers and late developers as a form of ecological reparation for past wrongs. The basic contours of this claim are certainly well attested, and in their recent book *A History of the World in Seven Cheap Things* Moore and Patel develop the thought that the 'modern world happened because externalities struck back'.[9]

They focus on the frontiers of early capitalist development, where the intersectional zones of empire, resistance and colonialism overlapped, and where technological adaptation (often of the most brutal kind) used non-white bodies as the very fuel for modern profits. Through this, they find in sixteenth-century English and Spanish expansion as well as the conquest of the Indies and the subsequent rise of the commercial Dutch Republic, the origins of a conceptual separation between the realm of the social or political and that of the natural. Descartes, for instance, is here given his own colonial epistemology (after serving as a soldier in Holland) as much as his sceptically individualist one, broadly because his argument is said to be derivative of a wider sense that the natural could be newly subjugated as separate from the human. So decoupled, the natural world could be controlled and utilized for (Godly) profiteering.[10] Here, slaves could be subjugated when redescribed as mere 'nature' rather than fully-fledged 'persons'; the by-now well-known doctrines of international law and hospitality could be used to justify warfare against apparent infidels; and techniques of extraction from the natural environment could be used against people as if they were worth less than the sugar cane they were made to harvest in Madeira.[11]

These interconnections track similar ecological webs throughout Moore and Patel's book: between finance (Genoese bankers), expansion (the Genoa-born Columbus) and this division between society and nature that relied upon the development of new technologies of appropriation and control (slavery and the 'extraction' of goods and profits from 'nature'). Once serially laid out, they are in a position to disinter the original force of a Marxist claim about the nature of capital as effectively a relationship of exploitation, like sophisticated analysts of class in long-term historical perspective have also done.[12] By so doing, moreover, they are more effectively able to highlight that the development of modern capitalism out of early modern absolutism underpins malignant legacies into the present, such as the buttressing of economic underdevelopment by forms of racial segregation or gendered hierarchies. The long-term perspective of this kind of argumentation underpins a wider sense of the continuing 'slow violence' of environmental exploitation and injustice that continues to affect great swathes of the global population.[13]

All this forms part of a broader concern with forms of capitalist 'ecology', that encompassing web of relations that has deep roots such that even the 'logic of twentieth-century state communism was struck in a sixteenth-century ecology'.[14] Each relies on a lowest-common-denominator approach to maximizing resources. Putting it more polemically, cutting costs and making everything cheap: cheap *nature*, which can be profited from with cheap *money* and cheap *work*, where *care* is cheap and life is fuelled by cheap *food*, all of which requires cheap *energy*, which in turn relies upon a broad conception of people with cheap *lives*. Through this global relationality, what Moore and Patel most provocatively claim is that capitalism has an inherently universalizing web, such that although European colonialism and expansionism was the original moment of capitalist development, capitalism, unlike its modern ideological coagulate, liberalism, is not inherently Eurocentric. It is necessarily global, and it sets to work first at the margins.

Once these connections are presented, however, it means in principle that there are ways in which the apparent 'losers' of these developmental tendencies across the centuries could be compensated through a form of ecological debt accounting, or 'reparation ecology'.[15] Such a perspective maps on well to critical discussions of reparations for past injustices at the bar of race, class and gender most strikingly, because it shows how rectification must go beyond the merely pecuniary.[16] It involves a political claim, straddling generations and time-frames, and is therefore a form of acknowledgement that needs to be woven into the very fabric of political societies and continuously updated. That means it presumes the construction of a 'representative claim', which demands something of representative politicians as well as those whom they represent. The debt such representatives owe to those whom they represent, at least in those countries who signed up to the 2015 Paris Summit, and which in turn requires the support of those in whose name action is to take place, is the construction of a national plan of action around climate change. The complexities of such claim-making in the combined contexts of local and global spaces with unjust pasts, and the determination of ecological 'co-benefits' as well as surrogate options in the present, makes it very difficult to generate any political agreement.[17]

Combining representative claim-making with a focus on ecological indebtedness nonetheless offers something old as well as something new. It is old to the extent that, rather like the major debates about reconstruction emerging after the First World War, political and economic logics of indebtedness generate different national and international dilemmas. But it is new in that the indebtedness we are interested in is now much broader, ecological rather than merely economic, and goes beyond the terrain established for most political theorists interested in these questions, such as whether John Rawls or Robert Nozick had the more compelling argument about self-ownership and just acquisition, or whether a sense of justice could be transmitted between generations. For both, a 'realistic utopia' was the goal of liberal politics; they just differed about what both terms might mean.[18] But can the overlapping temporalities of past, present and future, which combine in different ways across Anthropocene time and political time, accommodate past injustice understood from the perspective of climate change, and could a new, 'realistic' utopia about debt emerge out of these discussions?[19]

This is a powerful problem, and one that intersects directly with one of the near-clichéd challenges of Anthropocene time for modern politics, namely that it might even be easier to imagine the end of the world than it is to imagine changing the system of capitalism that has brought on climate crisis.[20] Those who benefit most at the level of high politics from the current global system tend to be the already structurally privileged members of global networks connecting the wealthy and powerful with those institutions that stand as markers of cultural prestige, and also often those ubiquitously referred to as the top '1%' of high income earners. In the era of the Anthropocene, however, might it be from this very elite who benefit from entrenched privilege and the maintenance of inequality that the most immediate hope for dealing with the challenges of climate catastrophe is to be found? This is part of a question implied in a recent book, Geoff Mann and Joel Wainwright's *Climate Leviathan*.

For its authors, the elaboration of a 'Climate Leviathan', akin to a world state but of interconnecting territories with a shared interest in maintaining a global system of inequality, might be able to meet some of the challenges of climate change; but perhaps for no other reason than as a by-product of the desire among its wealthy and privileged to continue to replicate their status over time. A more radical version of this, of course, is that *if* structures are capable of being advanced and curated for such ends in the first place, of doing more than merely espousing a politics of good intentions through the UN, for example, then the hegemony of this global elite might itself eventually come to be challenged by more democratic forms of control. Climate Leviathan might then be seen as a sort of transitional arrangement, rather like the old Marxist idea of the dictatorship of the proletariat, a pathway along the route towards a more just future. Instead of a vanguard party of revolutionary cadres, though, the vanguard now is the dominant elite or class, acting in their own self-interest.

While Climate Leviathan is one plausible extrapolation from contemporary international organizations and structures towards a form of planetary sovereignty, a 'reactionary' form of 'Climate Behemoth' that rejects such a planetary focus is another. 'Climate X' is a more radical, non-capitalist and anti-sovereignty model of politics that extrapolates from contemporary trends towards a future with democratic possibilities. This would be a new 'assemblage', perhaps, that could save the 'multitude'.[21] In similar vein, another plausible imaginary where climate change and the Anthropocene sit at the heart of political life could be a return to national self-sufficiency within the confines of nation-state boundaries: another version of the 'closed commercial state' model such as that once taken up by Keynes in the 1930s when responding to an imbalanced global order of Nazis, Bolsheviks, fascists, anti-fascists and imperialists. That was another world in which liberal politics had clearly 'failed' to conquer the

Malthusian 'devils' of unemployment and overpopulation.[22] Finally, a fourth option canvassed by Mann and Wainwright, 'Climate Mao', consists of a regional grouping of like-minded states and institutional hierarchies with a shared 'anti-capitalist' mentality, could seek to direct itself towards its own interest in securing its regions from the rash assault of industrial deprivation.[23]

If the future political conflicts of the Anthropocene occur somewhere within and between these models, they nevertheless track the more general sense, developed by Lonnie Thompson, that the three modes or responses to global climate change are always forms of *mitigation, adaptation* or *suffering*.[24] It suggests that statist or internationalist responses will also have to follow such modes, but further claims that in so doing, they are open to conflict and competition because all at least are straightforwardly political responses and strategies, and they can always change and adapt.[25] This is not always positive, of course, as a look at the recent Environmental Protection Agency website of the US government shows. After Trump's avowed rejection of the Paris agreements on climate change, whatever one thinks of them, the 2017 EPA website was taken offline to be 'updated', and now exists only as a mirror historical site. The 'updated' version has views about the environment and climate change that are, it seems, more in line with the views of the current administration.[26] A useful corollary of all of this is the recognition that there is nothing 'natural' about any of these responses at all. They are all political choices, and the principal barrier to an open discussion and calibration of these political choices is the predominance of a broad set of intellectual justifications, or ideological conventions, that present only certain ways of doing politics as natural or desirable. An Anthropocened politics must be a politics of anti-fatalism, and a space of open-ended political choice-making and claim-making, one that pursues conventional strategies of mitigation and adaptation where it can, but which frames the political time of the Anthropocene more expansively whenever possible.

Here, one thinks obviously of the legitimating ideological mantles of liberalism, democracy, managed capitalism, and so on and so forth, as the kind of reified abstractions that

naturalize certain approaches to political questions by delegit-
imating counter-narratives and counter-concepts. This is why
the push to historicize routinely comes with a denaturing
agenda, and a genealogical claim about debunking extant
beliefs and certainties.[27] Whether or not such debunking
genealogies can actually change the status of our epistemic
beliefs about the world as we understand them is a vexed
philosophical problem. Most simply assume that genealogies
open up spaces for thinking about how ideas and practices
can be vindicated or judged at the bar of truthfulness,
depending upon how much epistemic trust we might have in
those whom we listen to.[28] But in politics, where epistemic
consistency is not always the most precious commodity,
debunking the claims of others, whether justifiably or not,
can routinely open up issue areas and policy spaces that were
previously closed. That is why the stakes are so high in terms
of how we narrate the relationship between politics and the
Anthropocene.

As those who write about the Anthropocene as a
constitutive part of global capitalism argue, the uneven
developmental tendencies that buttress both can be seen
first by looking to the margins or frontier spaces where new
waves of technological opportunity and cycles of investment
and profit are sought. When thinking about the political
ecology of the early modern 'Capitalocene', for instance,
Moore claims that just as surely as the credit and debt ledgers
of the early modern commercial and resource-rapacious
Dutch Republic were built on its extractive deployment of
Norwegian timber, this also placed Amsterdam at the centre
of a global ecological revolution.[29] Whether in the new
power accruing to Brazilian sugar growers thanks to Dutch
commercial networks, or the radical shift of emphasis in the
movement and sale of human chattel slaves from the Congo
and Angola, commercial, ecological and environmental transformations and transfers were all part of the same capitalist
ecology. These global and local connections here were very
clearly represented in Dutch art too. For example, at a recent
exhibition at the Hermitage in Amsterdam, under the rather
nondescript title of the 'Portrait Gallery of the Golden Age',
the curators not only brought together thirty massive civic
portraits known affectionately as the brothers and sisters

of Rembrandt's celebrated *The Night Watch*[30] they also showed how the wider visual representation of the closed civic world of guilds and burghers in Amsterdam, where trading rights and status hierarchies were rigidly enforced by religion and family connections, opened out from the city into the vast global networks of 'free' trade that made ports like Amsterdam so dazzlingly wealthy.[31] The foundational importance of such guilds and city organizations to wider thinking about political economy, natural resources and sustainability is well known.[32] The 'debt' to the environment owed by commerce was as obvious then as it is now. What has changed is that the debts owed by the beneficiaries of these original and early practices of resource extraction and trade to those who were exploited, and who have continued to suffer from climate change most obviously, are becoming increasingly widely recognized.

*

In part, this is because climate-related crises, with their continuing and bluntly obvious force, are nothing short of a global emergency even without any obvious or agreeable global solution. This much is clear. But anthropogenic climate change and its effects operate on what Elizabeth Kolberg neatly describes as 'global warming's back-loaded temporality'.[33] The crises and emergencies that hit today are the result of generational, sedimentary and even planetary system shifts that take time to manifest themselves in the actual occurrences that humans register as events. This makes it the archetypical 'perfect storm' for anyone interested in questions about the normative and evaluative relationship between human agency and the environment, as well as for scientific and public policy responses across interconnected timespans of past, present and future.

Today, Arctic scientists and climatologists are able to determine even millennia-old carbon dioxide levels by dating and testing water frozen deep in the earliest available ice sheets. Such testing also lay behind the initial claim for Anthropocene time as an eighteenth-century development.[34] The calibration of levels of historical carbon can be both quantified and then set against developmental histories of unequal carbon-infused growth based on a (normatively, highly contestable) criterion of 'acceptable use'. Doing so, whatever the problems involved, allows for the construction of an 'historical emission's debt'.[35] It also compels a discussion about the entitlements owed to those who have been unfairly and unjustly treated by the past actions of others, actions that were undertaken without their consent, but which have imposed costs upon them.[36] It continues to show, unsurprisingly, that over the long run, historical emissions from India and China (extremely heavy polluters today) pale in comparison with the carbon indebtedness of the United States and Britain.

This need not militate against the construction of more just and environmentally sensitive, or Anthropocene-sensitive, carbon markets.[37] But it does make some heavy presumptions about the fact that collective agents can be identified and held accountable for emissions and pollution, while requiring some acceptance of the claim that we are all involved in a common enterprise regarding the earth's resources. This might hold true for cosmopolitan visions of the environment as a shared global good, though that's certainly not a universal view. Nor does this avoid traditional problems of power and inequality inherent in the relationship between ecological and economic debt in terms of *Realpolitik*. Consider, for example, Malaysia's recent attempt to break free of loans from China so as to avoid what its new leader considers to be potentially another form of 'debt colonialism'.[38] Or Yannis Varoufakis's account of Greek subjugation under the banner of EU-inspired austerity, which deploys a similar analysis to make sense of the financial crisis in Greece. In his view, the very recent suggestion that such austerity has ended, while debts continue to accrue for another fifty years, is little more than a straightforward lie because Greece was never bailed out at all.[39]

The question of Anglo-American indebtedness most obviously lies behind the fractious debates about intergenerational and international responsibility, uneven debts and economic growth that have been part of climate debates since the 1970s. As more recent scholarship has unravelled its political and intellectual history, the call by a pan-regional group of states in the global South for a New International

Economic Order in the 1970s has been seen to be crucial to the first phase of thinking about reversing the arrow of indebtedness. Building on earlier pan-African federal ideas about how to transition out of colonialism and into a future that would avoid the scleroses and colonial imaginaries of Northern 'nation-state' models of politics, the NIEO and the 1955 Bandung Conference offered alternative spaces for thinking about global indebtedness and interconnection.[40] Similarly, in Eastern Europe, particularly in states like Yugoslavia, debates about ecology and national autonomy were part and parcel of a combined attempt to think outside the confines of Soviet categories of modernity.[41] And yet the broad logic of a transition towards post-communism in many former Eastern bloc countries may well have had more consequential effects on reducing emissions by reducing forms of economic 'slack' than any environmentally conscious policy aimed at doing so.[42] Such unintended consequences that result from economic decline matter hugely. But for my purposes, it is enough to note that issues of ecological debt and indebtedness were most directly put on the table for modern audiences in the 1992 Rio Summit, and particularly its associated 'Debt Treaty'. This focused attention on the historical results of unequal trade between the global North and global South and redescribed the concept and language of debt in ways that an Anthropocened politics can make use of, as it continues to rewrite and revise the history of alternatives to nation-state politics.

Instead of being indebted to capitalist institutions like the World Bank and the International Monetary Fund, the conceptual innovation of the Debt Report was to make the global North into the recalcitrant debtor who would not pay what it owed for the early advantages it had unjustly acquired. Moreover, the debt here was more than monetary. As an 'ecological' debt, it concerned the use and exploitation of resources in the most capacious sense of that term, and thus offered a way of conceiving of restitution along various axes: biophysical, ecological and the normatively loaded criterion of environmental justice.[43] When considering ecological debt, economists have readily configured ways of assessing the cost of negative externalities and how these should motivate a 'polluter pays' principle, even though philosophers have cast doubt on the possibility of adequately identifying who should pay, and when.[44] Forms of negative tax are commonplace, although the wider contours of how best to utilize the national dividend for progressive public purposes, the question that so worried Pigou and his colleagues in the early twentieth century, is less often remembered today.

But that is precisely what writers in the later 1960s and early 1970s were trying to remember amid their own financial, environmental and population-based challenges. Then, radical appraisals of political and economic options about debt and growth were most certainly 'on the table', as we have already seen, and what was discussed in the early 1970s in the most general terms of relevance to Anthropocene narratives was an idea of there being 'social' and 'epistemological' as well as 'practical' limits to growth. Those limits might be transcended from time to time by technological advance and resource development that either challenges, or chimes with, major geopolitical relations.

Attempts to reverse debt's arrow were themselves part of a wider global moment of decolonization, which deployed anti-colonial critiques of the mirage of sovereign equality between states, a mirage that remains such a fixture of the ideologies of liberal internationalism and global governance that continue to try to remake the world in their own image today.[45] The concept of ecological debt, however, signals a wider set of distributional conflicts that come out of both unequal ecological exchanges in the past, and the tendency of wealthy countries to have disproportionately utilized environmental space without paying for its ecological costs in the present.[46] It has other radical implications. At one extreme, what has come to be termed as eco-terrorism (a label that is itself a political imposition, by states, about particular groups) might be thought a just response to unjust arrangements where previous debts from an unequal past have not been paid. The destruction of pipelines and fracking sites is one way in which this has developed, and itself marks a conceptual innovation in the language of debt or indebtedness, focusing on both what the problem is, and who is responsible for it. Without wishing to conflate so-called 'eco-terrorism' and activism with other forms of politically motivated terrorism necessarily, one pertinent claim that unites both is a radical assumption about the responsibility of those who represent, as well as those who are represented by, particular companies, states and regimes. Everything happens 'in your name' in this scenario, because state action is a direct consequence of popular will, or popular sovereignty. This direct responsibility is a much more democratic rendering of representative politics than most of those who inhabit representative democracies ever consider, except in moments of crisis and war.[47] And while, for some, environmental activism (and, by extension, Anthropocene time) is part of a war for the planet, to the contrary, the war against environmental activists and avowed eco-terrorists is commonly presented as a routine element of statist security strategies.[48]

This sense of acting in the name of, and being complicit in the actions of, your state, makes representation sound like a form of guilt which one should pay a penalty for when something goes wrong. This makes it less surprising that lawyers are also interested in the criminality or otherwise of ecological exploitation, wondering if the failure to act appropriately with resources could be an ecological crime.[49] In fact, a look at the Germanic terminology of debt helps to clarify this double meaning, because the concept of a debt (*Schuld*) here can both be pecuniary and simultaneously signal guilt. The imbrication of these terms, guilt and debt, then sounds an alarm, for there is often a dangerous moralism that surrounds discussions of both. This is what Nietzsche, who most infamously combined the terms, used to justify his claim that genealogy and historical forms of philosophizing offered the best form of critique against unjustly naturalized concepts.[50]

The Anthropocene has clearly already become such a concept about which there is only argument, and the interconnected concepts of ecological debt and indebtedness are equally only understandable from the point of view of their expression in forms of utterance and discussion, and therefore as forms of political argument and action. Sabotage of those elements in the modern Anthropocene that represent instances of guilt over the climate change that energy politics has wrought, and the debts that those who prosper from it are still to pay, forms part of a justificatory narrative for critics of major corporations and governments that look the other way when faced with environmental problems.[51] Unsurprisingly, however, this is also a new way of talking about very old dilemmas. Once again, we find a similar situation in the immediate aftermath of the First World War, when the outlawing of sedition and syndicalism, and crackdowns on revolutionary politics in general, were designed to render illegal even the mere expression of ideas about changing the political system. Under such circumstances, resistance and the fracturing of conventional discourses offer at the least an understandable response to an otherwise indifferent world.

That thought also motivated early twentieth-century responses to the rise of oil power as the new form of modern energy based around future-oriented considerations of geopolitics and American hegemony.[52] More pointedly, during the transition to a modern oil-powered economy, pipelines were sabotaged by angry workers whose collective bargaining power had been removed by new techniques of production as much as the distributional needs of consumers in the transition from coal. With the removal from coal mines of large numbers of workers whose capacity was physically required, which had granted veto powers of exit and bargaining, correlatively new forms of producer-driven forecasting also emerged.[53]

While this 'economentality' looked at production as a flow, seeing the economy as network and flow was not itself new. The very idea of a 'world economy' at the beginning of the twentieth century was a novel field of inquiry, but its pioneering figures looked to understand the dense locational and spatial networks that moved from individual connections to global patterns. What they ended up with in diagrammatic terms looked rather like a spirograph representation of intricate interconnection. Where does this leave us in our search for the idea of the Anthropocene as a spur to the notion of ecological debt? Not very far if we continue to buttress our politics with traditional energy regimes. But must we do so?

Adapting Helm's approach once more, what is interesting in the context of arguments about debt is that he suggests debt-financed borrowing for climate change is impossible. The 'war' against climate change will have to be fought and paid for differently. Instead, and more straightforwardly, taxation on consumption will need to be radically increased in order to motivate support for income-driven substitutional goods, and alongside this, there will also need to be an increase in taxation for environmental policy options. This mirrors Solow's earlier version of the problem, wherein he thought that a 'scarce resource' which is collectively 'owned', namely 'the waste-disposal capacity of the environment', is precisely what 'goes unpriced', and that, too, is something that politics could fix in conventional terms.[54] Through international trade, something like a carbon import duty on goods would be taken at the border of the receiving country. Preferably, and in order to avoid these border adjustments, traders would be 'nudged' to generate their own carbon efficiencies prior to shipping goods to market, and thus avoid the hit on their own profits that would be taken elsewhere as they moved their products around. When considered in the round, this sort of bottom-up rather than top-down international agreement-style model of redistribution has a much more impactful chance of generating a global engagement if our politics stays as it is, because it focuses as much on consumption as production. It also deals with the fact that large states like the USA are able to offset their carbon emissions much more effectively than others, in part because they did not sign up to Kyoto, but also because in the aggregate they trade less internationally than, say, the EU. This at least tackles a real political problem, that because democratic politicians have to be elected by consumers, consumers are the people who will have to pay, monetarily as well as metaphorically, for their choices. Once again, politicians will need to explain to people why they will have to pay more for less, and do so in a way that people will still vote for them. That is their task. It remains ours to hold them to account when they deceive us into believing in a mythical world of painless choices and perpetual growth, and to push them into serious discussion of these difficult choices. Perhaps no area in this connection is as morally fraught as population.

5

Population Futures

Moral and political philosophy is not the sort of science that can tell you exactly when and where the thresholds for action are, in the face of the numerous challenges raised by the Anthropocene. This makes the challenge of population in the Anthropocene a particularly tricky problem.[1] For population matters for modern debates about politics and the Anthropocene in at least two ways, neither of which suggest any straightforward connection between population size and political action. First, it does so in the rather obvious sense that the Anthropocene forces us to consider how human populations have changed their environments across different scales and extents, but in ways they might no longer be able to respond or adapt to.

Ironically, there seems to be some truth to the thought that had right-wing Christian narratives about stewardship of the earth gained greater traction with the evangelical revival of the 1970s and 1980s than, say, 'family values', this could have had some fairly positive results for offsetting climate change.[2] As one major recent essay has claimed, if the central question that matters is why, when there was the chance for it, international action failed to materialize in the decade of possibility, from 1979 to 1989, then the failures of the religious right in the United States might have had something to do with this.[3] Similarly, the language of co-benefit that is part and parcel of contemporary environmental politics (such that tackling environmental problems around housing, for example, might have co-benefits in terms of ameliorating certain forms of inequality) is also pertinent. It makes sense of the longer histories of environmentalism and environmental activism that align with traditions of civil disobedience (e.g. various forms of Red–Green alliance in campaigns for nuclear disarmament) and the often-romantic defence of wild places and spaces, particularly prominent within the modern United States from Thoreau onwards.[4] But the challenge of the Anthropocene for population takes us beyond narratives of stewardship and co-benefits.

The second reason why population matters to politics and the Anthropocene is actually more like two interrelated problems. One concerns the question of whether or not this particular planet and its ecosystems can readily support the activities of an increasing and expanding human population, which continues to rely upon fossil fuels for energy.[5] From 1750 to 1950, under a coal regime, the world's population grew by 1%. From 1950, with oil, that population rose by 2%, and since 1950 there has been peak growth, with the population increasing by nearly a billion every twelve to fifteen years. The other side of this issue has to do with the connection between population size and quality of life. What, then, are the 'limits', if any, to population across these various levels, and how might consideration of them help us to think about politics in Anthropocene time?

Towards the end of the 1960s, debates about population, or more specifically overpopulation, began to re-emerge in public discourse, in another generational iteration of an ongoing set of debates across the twentieth century.[6] The sense that planet Earth could not reliably accommodate projected demographic rates of increase led many to redeem the figure of Thomas Malthus, the second edition of whose *Essay on the Principles of Population* has long been a touchstone for demographically inclined historians and political theorists. The language of a population 'bomb', ticking and ready to blow, was part and parcel of mainstream discussion in the scientific and literary magazines of the period. Biological theories of change without the presupposition of moral progress or natural stability, Bay Area communalism in California and anti-colonial independence struggles in Asia and the Pacific as well as in Northern Africa most obviously, as well as student radicalism and Cold War standoffs in Europe, all produced a bewildering variety of discussions about population politics in the midst of seeming chaos and imbalance.

A raft of metaphors emerged to signal a concern with the condition of 'lifeboat' earth, or 'spaceship' earth, and the so-called 'tragedy of the commons' posed by rapid population growth and territorial movements. While scientists and public intellectuals worried about the aggregate population and finite resources, political philosophers wondered about how the important contexts of civil rights struggles, famine, migration and war affect our ability to measure the quality of life within and between populations, and how we should think about justice within and between generations. Marxists retained an interest in the big-picture political contexts. Less obviously but not unimportantly, many Western Marxists and independently minded area studies experts in anthropology began to look to a longer-term study of agrarian history for alternatives to modern capitalist states that seemed politically and intellectually moribund. At this time, agrarian studies departments in universities began to emerge in earnest, producing studies concerned with 'peasant' or 'tributary' modes of production prior to capitalism, and committed to uncovering histories of injustice, revolt and the so-called 'peoples without history'. Such topics have long since become mainstream.[7] Looking back, it seems as if the wide-lens comparative historical sociology of figures like Max Weber, interested in explaining what he saw as the uniqueness of Western rationalism and capitalism in global perspective, had begun to be taken seriously by contemporary Marxism, too.[8] The most public voices heard, though, were those of the natural scientists.

In Paul Ehrlich's famous book *The Population Bomb*, population numbers were tied to a claim about the need for there to be adequate resources for the entire, aggregated human population. Barbara Ward, followed by Kenneth Boulding, soon after popularized the idea of 'spaceship earth' as a place of finite resources, as population growth began to outstrip food supply and led to a resurgence of neo-Malthusian panics and projections. To some extent, all this built on a well-established series of moves in modern environmental and policy sciences linking the United States and the Soviet Union much earlier in the century. Then, consideration of the environmental systems within which planet Earth was embedded framed policy options geared towards economic development, but also a sense of the inter-connected and systemic character of policy, politics and the environment in a world of superpower rivalry.

This is also to say that the history of human population and earth system science in the twentieth century was from the outset an argument about how to plan for and manage resources into logically and systemically predicted futures as rational or ideological responses to an irrational and imbal-anced or unstable global order. Overpopulation threatened to knock these plans off track and, when aligned with other systemic crises, led writers like Ehrlich to predict a series of rather desperate scenarios towards the end of the 1960s. Here, food riots, international anarchy and nuclear attacks seemed likely outcomes of distributional conflicts over resources. At best, there was the possibility of cultivating new spaces out of which the victims of famine and violence could become the wards of a new international order, one based on technical expertise. This managed or curatorial care for the global population was one way in which a sense of balance could be restored, and where nobody rocked the boat, as it were, because it was carrying all the peoples of the world.

Such language of boats and ships, whether intergalactic or ocean-dwelling, was renewed in yet another metaphor about the construction of 'lifeboat earth'. On this lifeboat, however, not everyone could be saved without a precipitous decline in the standards of late modern prosperity and growth. Given that this was undesirable, population regulation and control seemed like an obvious solution to many. Garrett Hardin's famous analysis, beginning with the discussion of the 'tragedy of the commons' – wherein it was presumed to be impossible for resource users to overcome problems of collective action by means of cooperation – rendered the only solution as the imposition of either private or public ownership. He then moved further towards a claim about the necessity of living within ecological limits, suggesting ecological responsibility went hand in hand with conservatism about breeding and, latterly, the appropriate husbanding of domestic resources for continued planetary survival. If the ecosphere and its use *was* akin to a global commons problem, namely that the earth was being overgrazed by human beings, then at the aggregate level, he claimed the rational response to 'lifeboat earth' was a reduction in the global population to more manageable levels, whatever these might be.

Without any obvious agency to authorize such a move, at least in Western democracies, the problem of who 'speaks for' or 'acts in the name of' – that is, who 'represents' – both 'humanity' and the 'environment' arose once again. For many, such a problem could only be solved, or at best mitigated, by nation-states doubling down on their quest to govern those bits of the earth's territories that they happened to control. This might mean giving up on the idea of the earth as a 'global commons' or shared treasury for all, and seeing it instead as a series of discretely ordered locations and spaces within which different states or private entities governed particular resources and took care of their own populations. Instead of thinking about population through the metrics of an aggregating calculus associated with utilitarian moral philosophy (crassly restated as the greatest happiness of the greatest number, where *both* happiness and number matter), Hardin turned towards the relationship between population and the good life. Put another way, these developments led to a consideration of questions to do with population as themselves bound up with issues to do with quality of life and the moral standing of persons, or their personhood. It was, in Hardin's own iteration of the issue, a deeply divisive argument, for it classified peoples and persons with reference to the 'quality' of their lives or otherwise, and in his analysis, this could be linked to their race and ethnicity.[9]

Elinor Ostrom, among others, rather than giving up on the idea of the earth as a commons because of the impossibility of rational cooperation, set herself the challenge instead to produce more rational schemes of mutually advantageous cooperation that could deal with shared resource constraints and dilemmas, or 'common pool resources'. For this, Ostrom worked to understand how some historical schemes and structures of cooperation (e.g. fisheries or irrigation systems) had in fact been able to get around the impossibility conditions for cooperation established by Hardin, and why others had failed.[10] Having outlined the possibility of rational governance of commons problems (and a schematic reportage of which institutional forms had worked where and when), she won a Nobel Prize for her pathbreaking work. But these sorts of macro-social arguments about rational cooperation were not the only ways in which political thought came to grips with the problem of population and the question of the environment, or latterly the Anthropocene. Equally setting himself against figures like Hardin, John Broome maintains that the environment is a 'global commons', and because of this, governments have a duty to act to maintain its resources. Moreover, because they have to act in situations where new information leads to new public goods problems and so forth, he suggested that if utilitarianism dropped its own assumptions of neutrality about the addition of new members to a global population set and considered more thoroughly how many people the global commons could support, we might come to think about valuing population on the grounds of the responsibilities, rather than the potentialities, of future people, and about the restitution of past injustice by present peoples.[11] To develop his claims, Broome proposed a teleological theory with an account of the good life at its heart that peoples across time and space can share, and one that gives us reasons not to harm others. This he called a more 'complete utilitarianism'.[12]

*

Some more obvious ways in which population talk remains a fraught area for the politics of the Anthropocene come from historical connections between population control and eugenics, racial slavery and neo-Malthusian dilemmas about resources. For liberals, there is a further concern that somehow the governing of populations smacks of an intervention into the private sphere of individuals that is normatively unappealing and practically undesirable across many levels, even if, as Michel Foucault famously suggested, liberalism emerged through concrete practices and strategies of what he called 'governmentality', strategies explicitly bound up with controlling, regulating, managing and hygienically cleansing 'populations' for modern 'society'.[13] Nevertheless, following Diana Coole, we can see that population politics in political theory has often been submerged at the level of narrative, and that discursive strategies for dealing with, or rather for avoiding, population talk come in different styles.

These are, variously, population shaming (where the discussion struggles to move beyond entrenched epistemological limitations fostered by unequal North–South relations of colonial exploitation and racism), population scepticism (demographic transition theory prompts scepticism about rising population), population declinism (which builds on scepticism to claim that populations are actually lowering, but focuses only on the short run), population decomposing (not referring to aggregate levels of population and welfare as 'other-regarding', but instead seeing population as a self-regarding activity to do with choice and individual liberty) and population fatalism (suggesting that it's not something that can readily be factored into debates about climate change and the Anthropocene).[14] Obviously, attempts to discuss population control and regulation across the global North and global South play very differently depending upon where you start from, and they often in fact mirror the prior claims about unequal development and historical injustice that prompt the claim about debts and burdens discussed elsewhere.

During many moments of tension in the 1960s and 1970s, normative debates about population bifurcated into at least three further, related strands. One set of debates turned to questions of international or global justice, asking what, if any, duties states had to alleviate humanitarian disasters, natural emergencies and threats that affected non-national populations. Central figures in political philosophy here were Peter Singer, Onora Nell, Brian Barry, Charles Beitz and their successors. They challenged the rather blunt edges of Hardin's preference for the lifeboat and the rather serene philosophical discussion of rights and duties that, as Nell sardonically quipped, often seemed to think about rights and duties to populations as if they were like the problem of whether or not one was allowed to step on the lawns in an Oxbridge college.[15] Instead, these debates (which effectively began to internationalize Rawls's basic sense of justice as rational cooperation under conditions of uncertainty) strengthened the view of those who thought of the earth as a spaceship. This vessel was, and is, capable of saving the many, but only if the right institutions and sets of human duties could be made to align. A related concern about migration mixed within both of these strands, often also combining Christian and conservative presumptions, asking whether or not there were human rights of assistance and care that prompted particular international responses to human rights abuses.[16] In our contemporary moment, with still further and massive global migration crises unevenly scattering displaced persons, fragmenting families and challenging old-fashioned justifications for national boundaries, such concerns have returned under the auspices of questions about whether democratic societies have any 'right' to police and control their borders, or if they have a 'duty' to keep them open, or whether citizenship really requires more than merely residence.[17]

Numbers speak loudly in all these cases, and the aggregate figures of population growth are certainly staggering. From a global population of 2.5 billion in 1950, which doubled to 5 billion in 1990, by 2020 it is expected to have tripled, culminating in a population of some 10 billion or more at the end of this century. Just searching online about the question of limits to population also brings up a whole raft of discussion, from David Attenborough to radical fringe groups, suggesting that the planet simply cannot accommodate as many people as are predicted to be born, to others who advocate extreme forms of population management and control. For those interested in a sort of Anthropocened politics, the problem of population goes beyond the merely numerical once again, because as the backward temporalities of past climate change play out and become increasingly obvious in the present, their future implications will become increasingly difficult to legislate around.

This in fact is where we already seem to be in terms of climate change. Pick any date almost at random over the past two years, consult the news archives, and you'll find numerous climate-related crises and disasters to consider, from New York to Haiti, India and Indonesia to Japan, Senegal to the Yemen, across every continent and every coastline. Rising sea levels, increased acidification, melting glaciers, tidal waves, oil spills, earthquakes, volcanic eruption, power outages, energy chaos: the list is practically endless, and most of it is outside of any kind of human control, even while we might recognize that human action across various temporal boundaries past and present has been a contributing factor in 'causing' such events. As Andreas Malm puts it, we are already in the middle of a climate storm, making ours an era of near-permanent environmental crisis. It neatly matches, with some bathos, the seemingly permanent age of scandal also affecting global politics since the 1970s.[18]

For critically minded political theorists, this invokes at least two further connections between population and modern politics. The first is that the languages of both political time and Anthropocene time are legacies of an eighteenth-century analysis of politics concerned with the conflict between nation-states and domestic populations in practice, and the normative idea of a shared humanity connecting the peoples of the world. The age of the nation-state, it seems in prospect as well as in retrospect, has been an age of permanent crisis over this division as much as it has been an age of increased welfare, health, age and prosperity. For many writers, like Carl Schmitt and Reinhart Koselleck (whom Schmitt influenced as a younger man), this meant that modern appeals to 'humanity' in modern politics were little more than a moralized mirage. Often they cause a permanent breach in the fissures of political possibilities, dramatizing moral responses to practical dilemmas, but relegating their resolution to an undefined point in an unanticipated future. Nation-state-based politics, by contrast, with somewhat clearer lines of sovereignty and accountability, track more directly the need for an authoritative locus of decision-making authority. This is a schematic opposition or binary view of modern politics, but it points to something interesting, because it mirrors the criticism both Schmitt and Koselleck also made of Marx's analysis of the idea of a dictatorship of the proletariat. There, a solution is plausible that will be better for humanity, but one can't say when it will come. It is a hope postponed until the time is ripe and there is an institutional configuration that can deliver for humanity. In parallel, functional inter-nationalist organizations like the League of Nations or the

United Nations similarly appeal to humanity. But in the eyes of critics like Schmitt and Koselleck (perhaps unsurprisingly, given their own experience of German occupation), they often really act to buttress imperialist control by the old order.

For Marxian writers and activists, the prospective trope supplies perennial grounds for optimism about the open-ended qualities of politics going forward, even if the resultant transformation might require a sort of theoretical fatalism. How could things be otherwise if the systemic architecture has been correctly understood? For critics, the appeal to the interests of humanity is simply a cheat, a non-argument that merely sounds like one, presuming a mythically unified agency that will bring about a better world at some indeterminate point in the future. For both, however, the rise of the modern nation-state and its claims to sovereignty has fixed this tension as the central issue for representative politics, and in large part that remains the defining presumption behind the idea that modern nation-states are the major sites through which global problems must ultimately be considered.[19] It is why we still need to think about the relationships between domestic, international and global politics, with their conflicting norms, values, hierarchies and debts, when we consider the disconnect between the theory and practice of coordinated action to meet challenges like climate change. And here, new thinking about how spaces like the Arctic could become issues for future 'global' governance shows one way in which climate change might prompt new forms of international relations at least. Debates about the Anthropocene help to focus attention on these possible futures.[20]

In earlier twentieth-century versions of these discussions, Marxist critics like Rosa Luxemburg and Walter Benjamin targeted modern capitalism itself as the source of permanent catastrophe through war, economic crisis, imperialism and colonialism. The only way to see this was by looking backwards pessimistically, while moving forwards optimistically. This is why Benjamin surveyed what he saw as the wreckage of human history with Paul Klee's 1920 post-war work *Angelus Novus* as his pictorial guide. This is how he configured the angel of history, blown forward by a storm from

Paradise but whose face is turned toward the past, and who can thus only see history as perpetual barbarism, wreckage and chaos.[21] The only progressive options out of this vision were oppositional, requiring a choice between socialism or barbarism. Because capitalism makes catastrophism a permanent feature of everyday life on this reading, it can only be overcome with the transition towards socialism and the near-messianic promise that this involves of the possibility of a better life. In our own politics, this sometimes prompts another version of accelerationism, whereby the inherently contradictory tendencies of modern capitalist production, particularly automation and its distributive impact upon jobs requiring both very high- and very low-skilled labour, are pursued in order to speed up crisis tendencies and lead to new sorts of systemic resolutions. But it is the permanence of the catastrophe that renders the vision such an attractive heuristic for so many others who have come to think there is no resolution at all to be had, only the theologically driven 'hope' that something better is intrinsically possible. It might also, in fact, be a realistic vision of political possibility in modern democracies.[22]

It is perhaps unsurprising that the intellectual genealogy of Western Marxism in the 1960s and 1970s, particularly in the Anglophone world through the prism of *New Left Review*, was attacked for its apparent intellectual elitism and divergence from classical revolutionary politics in pursuing the ideas of writers like Gramsci and Benjamin very pointedly. But in so doing, these Western Marxists were offering their own responses to the seeming permanence of catastrophe under modern capitalism, supporting Third Worldism and cultivating a critical engagement with the study of development economics. This was also a space in which to curate new analyses of the ways in which race and structural racism made up part of the cultural and political hegemony of the modern state.[23] And such considerations were aligned with a related strand of post-Marxist thinking in France and Greece, through the work of people like Cornelius Castoriadis and Claude Lefort, who were both members of what was known as the *Socialisme ou Barbarie* collective. Their analysis of contemporary politics was to consider it a crisis of democracy, which moved them to reconfigure democracy as what Lefort called a 'theologico-political' problem.[24]

That's yet another claim with a complicated genealogy, but what it means in practice is that democracy becomes a promise, a more or less empty space or signifier (Lefort called it a *'lieu vide'*). It becomes a space for permanent hope, because it is something that can never actually be realized, a regulative ideal or promise (even a myth) to believe in, and against which to judge contemporary politics. Even if you think that democracy is a bloated, misunderstood and capaciously indiscreet term for talking about how what we call democratic politics actually functions in the modern world, this Francophone tradition nevertheless retains both a critical and an optimistic resonance.[25] And these responses to the permanence of catastrophism, alongside the increased interest of Marxist writers in the problems of environmental crisis as a consequence of capitalist crisis in the 1960s and 1970s, signalled another moment in the evolution of a 'rift' between 'nature', 'society' and population that was analogous to a form of war.[26] But it was anarcho-capitalist philosophers (like Jan Narveson) and other critics of utilitarian and Marxist forms of egalitarian 'levelling' (like Derek Parfit) who sought to challenge some of the implications of these views in terms of population discourse. Narveson in particular suggested that although it might be good to make people happy, it is only morally neutral to do so, and thus it is not directly action-guiding as a requirement that we make happy people.[27]

If the choice between socialism or barbarism was one between making people happy or making happy people, then only the former has motivational force. For Parfit, instead, the challenge of population involved complex philosophical issues to do with two major problems. The first was that personhood over time was not stable (he termed this the 'non-identity' problem). If I am literally not the same person in the future as I am now, if I lack the same 'identity', then how can my discounting the future into a value that makes sense in the present properly function? The second engaged him in a critique of the equalizing or levelling assumptions of utilitarianism and Marxism. This grounds upon which this matters concern whether we think equality (both of and between persons) is an absolute, or relative, value, and how we think about the 'neutrality' of adding more people to a population.[28] What, then, could possibly be wrong, asked Parfit, with what he termed the 'mere addition' of one person to a global population? According to utilitarian reasoning, where maximizing happiness for the maximum number is the end goal, it seems logical to assume that more people means more possible happiness. And yet, Parfit added, how many people makes for too many people, such that the model of the greatest happiness begins to break down? Surely, he wrote, without some other criteria, we could end up with what he called a 'repugnant conclusion'.

In Parfit's account, starting from the plausibility of merely adding one person to a population set without seeming to diminish the quality of life or maximizing of happiness within that set, we could continue to add, one at a time, until we end up with a situation in which there is a vastly expanded number of people, such that maximizing happiness for all has become impossible except at the most rudimentary level. That is to say, we could end up in a situation where a large population with a high quality of life, governed by the principle of maximizing welfare and pleasure for its members, is progressively watered down into a vastly larger population with a correspondingly lower quality of life, simply because we have failed to take cognizance of the problems posed by 'mere addition'. This repugnant conclusion is a soritical version of the claim made earlier by Hardin, about the need to prioritize moral reasoning about the quality of life over aggregate considerations of welfare. It matters, too, for dealing with environmental issues.[29]

Applied to energy policy and global warming effects on future generations, for example, Parfit latterly wanted to say that it was wrong to choose cheap energy in the present that would cause increased problems down the line for future generations and increase global warming. This was so not simply because it would have been better to choose policies in the present that would in turn cause different future people to exist and which would make things go better for them. Instead, the problem is that whichever people are caused to exist (which is always better for them in principle than not being born at all), things will go worse for them, or, put the other way around, they will lack the benefits that the better present policy would provide in the future, thanks to policy choices made in the present. That is enough to make it the wrong choice.

The question of population at the level of numbers and resources, on one side, and quality of life, on another, is clearly central to the sense that Anthropocene time has dissolved the distance between human agency and its ecological contexts. The non-identity problem and what Parfit came to think of as a 'wide', person-affecting viewpoint of moral decision-making focuses our attention on the question of whether it might sometimes, if not always, be better morally if fewer people were to have a greater quality of life than a much larger number who collectively produce a larger set of benefits both individual and collective, but who have a lower quality of life. But once we try to factor in the environmental contexts within which claims about quality of life necessarily occur, such issues become very broad-gauge indeed, albeit amenable perhaps to a more direct form of political judgement. For although we might never know exactly where vague thresholds lie, we can determine that action will need to be taken if we are to avoid various sorts of repugnant conclusions. And that is a political decision.

*

Discounting the future against the present is perhaps the best-known part of the economists' toolkit when it comes to thinking about climate change and these sorts of problems. Most are unfazed by Parfit's philosophical worries when discounting involves the production of a value on goods or currency and the like, and because evolution seems to show a natural capacity across species to adapt flexibly to 'typical' uncertainties moving forward.[30] In general terms, the higher the discount rate, the lower the value of the present to those considering it. In a review commissioned several years ago, for instance, Nicholas Stern proposed a social discount rate of between 1.4% and 2%, suggesting that this was the appropriate level of investment today in order to provide future generations with at least a similar set of distributed goods to those we currently have. Jam tomorrow, however, not only means paying a social discount rate for jam today of 1.4%. It also presumes a likely return upon that investment.[31] Others, like William Nordhaus, proposed nearer to 6%, which suggests both a higher risk and a higher degree of uncertainty about the outcome. The lower the discount rate, crudely put, the greater the value placed on the present; the higher the rate, the greater the value placed on the future and on future generations. What the debate about discount rate shows most forcefully, perhaps, is that political and economic choices are never just present-minded, as is borne out in the history of economic thinking.[32] By moving beyond presentism, even very technical debates can provide a service not often explicitly paraded as such by economists, because they demonstrate the folly of applying merely parochial and local time calculations (e.g. the metrics of election and news cycles) to major political and economic problems. By trying to factor in a number for cost–benefit analyses of whether or not to pursue future policies under conditions of disequilibrium and uncertainty, merely asking the questions helps to prevent debilitating fatalism.

What, then, is involved in the calculation of a social discount rate? The conventional view is that we should be interested in time preferences of individuals, and the social utility of projects both now and into the future, where costs can be discounted. However, discounting based on economic forecasting models also has to configure the ways in which additional demand for consumption can be subtracted from the overall unity of a population, to allow it to be transposed into each generation's 'felicity'. This generational felicity is the sum of its entire membership's 'felicity', which means that a time discount rate, plus the relative elasticity of felicity, forms the parameters of a model about how to make choices that can discount future preferences. But when we think about environmental justice between generations, for example, this raises the question of how to disaggregate wealth and income so as to understand the various welfare-relevant metrics that are bound up with environmental discount rates. To do this, most economists have to operate with modelled assumptions about a closed economy, and for environmental issues this seems problematic. For others, given epistemic uncertainty about both the present and the future, social discounting often seems insufficiently attentive to differences in value when it assumes that consumption rates are averaged both across and between similar individuals. Instead, an agent-relative discounting might be developed as what has been called a special case of 'hyperbolic time discounting', where the present (and individual preferences within the present) always trumps the future, but the future is weighted equally across *all* future generations, regardless of proximity. When appropriately Anthropocened, this 'felicity' is inserted into any calculation of a 'generation's well-being', and would have to be set against a hazard rate for global destruction as a possible threat moving into that future.[33]

For most of us, these technical questions of uncertainty and negligibility can nonetheless have a more immediate relevance. Should I bother recycling my waste properly? Will I make any perceptible difference to the desired outcome of reusing resources and reducing waste? Here, of course, there are difficult issues of causation and probability to think through, lying behind our often pessimistic musings about whether our own singular actions can make any difference, which might lead to an unwillingness even to try. After all, if my actions are irrelevant, why bother? Many philosophers and ethicists have shown that seriously imperceptible differences in effect (which is not the same thing as saying that the increment being added per person is imperceptible) do, however, magnify into collectively causal and perceptible change. If it really is in my interest to save the planet and I want to be part of bringing about that outcome, and my individually minuscule actions could in fact make some perceptible difference to the outcome, then I should act.

Conversely, even if I am interested in doing this but nobody else is, my individual agency will have no causal effect on the outcome, and there may then be no good reason for my doing it at all. That matters hugely, because if we do have the causal power to change our actions, then we might also have a responsibility to do so. But if as individuals we lack that power, then political representatives and corporate agents with great wealth and power might themselves have a cognate responsibility to act. This is where politics kicks back in, because if politicians recognize such claims as valid, then they may well have to admit to the responsibility they have to act and be judged, even if they cannot know exactly upon which environmental threshold their actions will, or won't, make a pivotal difference. Political judgement about this sort of terrain once again starts to look very much like a solution to the sorites paradox, in that causally effective political action not only requires a recognition of the vagueness of particular thresholds in achieving certain ends, but also requires a willingness to act in the face of that vagueness. Population seems very much like one of these problems, where vague thresholds permit a wide variety of interpretations as to whether and when political action should be taken. Such qualifications are magnified when we also recognize that any such action will only be causally efficacious if the relevant other parties who are required to act do in fact also act.[34] Moving our politicians to act in ways that might foster a new sort of Anthropocened politics both domestically and internationally, one that recognizes such complexities and responsibilities, but which also rejects fatalism, is clearly a major challenge. But it gets us to a necessary conclusion, that in order to understand the relationship between political time and Anthropocene time, we have to see it as a problem of value as much as scale.

6

Value

How might Anthropocened considerations of political value be fixed into normal politics? To take one major illustration, Partha Dasgupta has asked how environmental costs can be incorporated into national accounts in ways that are more sophisticated and coherent than, say, the simplifying measures of GDP. By so doing, he has tried to incorporate into the balance sheets a measure of both the intrinsic and functional worth of ecosystems with reference to their use value, intrinsic value and option value.[1] This means reconceiving of wealth in the widest possible terms, focusing on the distribution of assets across institutions, financial wealth and income, human capital and time, to curate a new accounting for value. Then, with this in mind, we find an alternative metric with which to consider how we might track inter-generational well-being over time for this newly defined wealth, and track concerns about sustainability in the present and into the future. In Dasgupta's reading, this is simply caching out what was implicit in Rawls's work on a just savings rate in the later 1960s and early 1970s, which political economists focused on but could not make work within the confines of the latter's wider system. Wealth and well-being, on Dasgupta's now broader canvas, allow us to consider questions of development and the rise and fall of nations as well as offering some pause to the usual sorts of discussion about the social discount rate.

Dasgupta's argument concludes with the thought that wealth must therefore be summed as the value of all the capital stock there has been in the past, which will make up the future and which is also part of an inter-generational calculus. From this perspective, we can determine a 'shadow value' so as to arrive at the price of comprehensive wealth thanks to a differently conceptualized account of inter-generational value, one that has quite radical implications for how we might think about a host of 'environmental' issues.[2] These range from the Pigovian route of taxing negative externalities through to the ways in which philanthropy and aid might transform societies into the future, focused around the stimulus for freedom prompted by economic development.[3]

We know how vexed philanthropy is as a route to independence and autonomy, especially after recent debates surrounding 'effective altruism'. It is hugely difficult to target aid, to have it arrive with the right people able to use it, in contexts wherein global supply chains are often precisely designed to keep in check those places and peoples who are part of the foundation of the carbon economy.[4] In order to think differently about these problems, there needs to be a rethinking about the values we place on persons (which is why I focused attention on writers like Parfit in the previous chapter) and on types of prosperity and growth.

*

What most commentators seem to think is that this first prompts the need for new 'narratives' with which to make sense of these common interconnections and complex ecologies between past, present and future. George Monbiot, for example, suggests that without an alternative shared narrative, culled from among the various other narratives this book has discussed, there can be no shared sense of politics. That implies, of course, that our current standard and shared narratives of neoliberal politics themselves are capable of being challenged; thinking they are not is simply to reify them. At the same time, deeper narratives about the environment as something external, to be used as a resource or husbanded according to need, even as the system that sustains human life, need to be repurposed such that they can become central to all ongoing discussions of Anthropocened politics.

If modern politics is to be Anthropocened, then this sort of 'narrative rinsing', as it were, is one part of the necessary process of cleaning up our political language and values. This can certainly help to ground it upon a new understanding of care, a sort of rather loose but collective answer to the problem once posed by Harry Frankfurt as the 'importance of what we care about'.[5] Frankfurt's account of individual persons with free will suggests that such persons can effectively pursue their first-order desires (meaning a desire to have something other than another desire) by acting according to second-order volitions. But he also offered a claim that what persons ultimately care about is what they love, and what they love and care for appropriately is themselves and their relations to others.[6] From this, what 'we' as collective and corporate political agents might 'love', beyond the breathless sense of the wild beauty of a (never) pure environment in the age of the Anthropocene, requires something else. It might mean taking responsibility for our own attitudes and dispositions by not only identifying with them, but also being judged as the sorts of agent capable of being held responsible for their conduct in public settings.[7] If that requires a narrative 'we' can believe in, in China Miéville's terms, it might actually necessitate a utopianism of the 'non-we', a radical challenge to the idea (much in vogue in the wake of the global financial crisis) that 'we' are all in it together. Recognizing the uneven distribution of costs and benefits of climate change and the Anthropocene might require a political strategy of manifest opposition and revolution.[8] For writers like Monbiot, such thinking means instead the transformation of political language in the first place, a full-bodied constructivism of the intellect amid a continued pessimism of the will. Yet the capacity for new narratives to compel allegiance will depend upon their resonance from past to present. This in part is what makes the current reappropriation of the language of a Green 'New Deal' in America championed by Alexandria Ocasio-Cortez so potentially enchanting, while in Britain, calls for a Green New Deal have a less canonical connection to a shared political imaginary.[9]

In part, though, what both approaches also call for is something we've seen before, particularly in the discussion of growth, namely a plea to prioritize both human and ecological value on different axes from merely capitalist profit. To do that, we need to learn how to 'see' the earth differently, to reconsider what it is that we should reasonably value in it, and to revisit the question of 'labour'. This can veer dangerously close to a pseudo-eschatological melodrama, wherein either Gaia or Mother Earth needs to be saved by her delinquent human children, or the end times are approaching, and all the human species can do now is learn how to die appropriately amid civilizational as well as ecological catastrophe.[10] Although politics does sometimes deal in apocalyptic and eschatological time, it does so usually only to show what the appropriate limits to civil politics in the here and now might be. That, at least, seems to be one lesson of modern representative politics: you get stable politics once you remove the threat of the end of days from daily political life, primarily by denaturalizing it.[11]

What we seem to require is a view of civil politics as both representative and artificial but simultaneously natural and Anthropocened, and this must mean being open to complexity, uncertainty and doubt, while avoiding the pathologies of fatalism. What sort of politics is capable of 'being ecological' in such a way at all? Well, so far only representative 'democratic' forms of politics look like they have the potential to be able to do this, at least in principle. In part, this is because of the claims that democracy is premised both on an open-ended hope into the future, and on a history of successful adaptability. The complex relationship between personality, rights and the attribution of action to non-human agents such as states and corporations in the history of modern democratic politics also offers some grounds for optimism, in that human beings might be able to meet the challenges of holding ourselves responsible when and if we choose to change how our politics works in relationship to mitigation, adaptation or suffering. Perhaps this resonates with Christopher Stone's claim about how to deal with rights of non-human objects in nature. For him, human beings should deal with them as one would deal with 'legal incompetents' in human relations, at least as a temporary strategy, until we learn more about those we share the planet with.[12] Perhaps, in the end, this is also just to make the claim that modern history and politics already *is* Anthropocened politics. For human ways of talking and acting politically, and our sense of modern history at least, are coterminous with the various times of the Anthropocene.

*

For others, the challenge of the Anthropocene for politics requires a human answer to the question of what the earth actually is, and that is something that has exercised political philosophers since the Great Acceleration, if not before. Technological change, and the concept of technology or 'technicity' as a form of ideology akin to a religious dogma, has, of course, both a long history and been subject to a large degree of historical criticism. It also has a singularly Christian dimension, but one which has spatial oddities. The idea of the 'globe' as both the shape and location of the 'earth' and simultaneously the centre of a divine system makes little locational sense. Either the world was made by a God who did not quite understand what they were doing because they put humans, after their own image, into a part of the galaxy that was certainly not its centre. Or, they rather oddly subsumed their own importance by locating themselves on the periphery of things, galactically speaking. Either way, as we have already seen, debates about centre and periphery, North and South, inside and outside, matter to the idea of the Anthropocene inasmuch as they frame how human beings see the location of the earth as a sphere, globe or home.

Timothy Clark suggests that what the Anthropocene does to our own narratives and visions of politics is to prompt a 'realization of the contingency of this normal [human] scale' of talking about ourselves as persons with agency in a rather traditional way. He pushes instead for a sort of 'ecophenomenology'.[13] This would avoid conflating 'earth' with 'world', 'planetary', and so forth. And his desire for specificity here takes us back to perhaps the most famous image associated with the Anthropocene and with planet Earth in general: the Earthrise image from Apollo 8 in 1968, and its follow-up

Earthrise (© NASA, 1968)

from Apollo 17 in 1972, the vision of terraqueous loneliness in the dark, known as 'Blue Marble'.

Such an image of a singular earth, a sort of 'defiant' vision of a planet standing alone, is challenged by the reality of Anthropocene time, the developing history of earth as part of a wider planetary ecosystem, as well as deep-time narrations of the geological past. But that challenge comes with an opportunity, one where humans come to see the world as something 'in the making', an ecology that does not require an 'eternal response' in terms of social and political organization, but which they can respond to creatively, by thinking anew about alternative forms of organization and value.[14]

Philosophers like Martin Heidegger famously thought that this sort of image was part of an ongoing destruction of the local by technology, whereby those local places in which the

Blue Marble (© NASA, 1972)

'being-there' (*Dasein*) of individuals really was rooted in a
sense of being home, where their being had some connection
to the earth, were gradually eroding.[15] Instead, what Earthrise
offered was the world as an image, a technically reproduced
image at that, reducing humankind from being grounded
beings with a place or a home in the world, to creatures
holding merely temporary membership status of a planet. For
others still, the Anthropocene signals a need to rethink the
nature of the earth as a planetary home, but with only finite
resources; indeed, resistance to Heideggerian-style pessimism
about the ineradicable loss of 'home' through technology will
certainly be a requirement of any Anthropocened politics.

When pressed by one of the most pungent contemporary
critics of a Christianized version of Gaia, Bruno Latour, this
becomes an argument about how the 'whole' of the earth is

actually rather 'less' than the sum of its parts. Latour pursues his claim about 'actor-network theory' into the debate about the Anthropocene, wherein the earth is a network of things (rather like the internet of things), each delicately connected but with no overarching 'whole' that makes sense of them. It therefore needs a 'parliament of things' to govern it.[16] What we need to see, he thinks, is that the Anthropocene poses a challenge akin to war for humankind and for earth, but in a time of (from Latour's European perspective) relative peace. In war, the struggle for survival requires an awareness of who the enemies and the peacemakers are, meaning that the 'earthbound' need to go to war for the sake of their own earth, which is a home made up of a network of things that each have value, that each create value, and that altogether are the only things that can have any value at all.[17] Here, 'being ecological' is the only game in town for modern realists and critics; it's just that we don't often see that there really is no other choice, which is why we need the new narrative about the value of earth to the earthbound.

The Anthropocene can provide us with the resources to think this through, but the fact that it is still so often presented as separable from mainstream global politics is what gives us pause. Latour has reiterated this in another, more recent book. He argues now that over the last two generations, the confluence of economic deregulation, increasing political and economic inequalities within states and the stand-off between climate change deniers and the brute realities of increasingly regular climate crises shows one thing clearly. Namely that climate change is, in fact, at the very heart of modern geopolitics, but that what we lack is a way of reconnecting the language of the earth (the geo- in geopolitics) to the idea of a shared world of values. The Anthropocene has updated our sense of 'ecology', and in so doing, it has made the planetary habitat political, or, rather, it has expanded the domain of the political into the 'terrestrial'. This 'terrestrial', in Latour's terms, has therefore become an 'actor' in its own right, a 'geo-' which is an 'agent that participates fully in public life'. The problem is that nobody as yet knows how it will act in this new, old world where everything connects, because humans have as yet no 'global' language and indeed scale for politics that can mobilize the terrestrial.[18] More importantly, nobody understands how the 'terrestrial' could in any obvious way be represented, or authorized, by any conventional political structures. The 'system' of political theory must be reconfigured to account for it, as many eco-democrats have long argued.[19]

Unsurprisingly, therefore, one of the main ways in which Anthropocene time enters political time is via a radical redescription of the politics and agency of non-human life. Here, if everything is connected, and if we are interested in the question of value, we might want to follow Donna Haraway in her bid to 'stay with the trouble', to think about what it means to be 'kin' with those with whom we cohabit the planet. This can at first appear dangerously close to a rampantly anti-political vision in the sense of any kind of collective politics that human beings have ever known. At the same time, however, it signals the extent of the challenge that we think about ourselves in the same way as we might think about 'critters' or 'dirt', for example. If context is everything, then just as to a worm the extent of its world is the extent of the material that surrounds it, then to human beings as well, the earth is similarly the network of connections and kin surrounding them. Here, planet Earth is not a self-regulating system, or, in the jargon of systems theory, autopoietic. Instead it is 'sympoietic', which is to say that to understand it requires a sense of interconnection and sympathy within and between its network of things. Thinking of the living entities who cohabit planet Earth alongside human beings might also prompt a quite radical challenge of what solidarity with other living things requires. Are those who 'work' here 'labourers', or 'comrades' even, with 'us'? Perhaps only an awareness of the hybrid qualities of politics and labour in the Anthropocene can reorient us towards a sense of shared values.[20]

The metaphor Haraway chooses for thinking this through is tentacular, and she calls it the Chthulucene, roughly speaking following the name of the Chthulu spider that inhabits the underside of trees in her neighbourhood. On her account, thinking about the value of the global is irrevocably a claim about the nature of the local and the interconnected, without any inter-species hierarchy.[21] For Haraway, like Latour, there is no space for the international politics of bargains and treaties here to be separate from the wider ecology that connects those who live together on planet Earth, because there is no 'outside' from which to judge questions of value or 'national' interest, for instance. Just as she had argued a generation earlier for a form of 'cyborg' feminism that could not be reduced to claims about gender, sexuality, need or desire, for Haraway today, a similarly cyborgian-sounding language of the Chthulucene (but which is not the same as H. P. Lovecraft's demonic Cthulu) might be the best way of responding politically to claims about value in the age of the Anthropocene.[22] It is one that requires human beings to learn that they really are the stuff that dreams are made of, where the materiality of the body and the psyche are intertwined, as she puts it, in ways that Foucault 'hardly dreamed of', though neurosurgeons and neuroscientists have been telling us this for a long time.[23]

Once again, the way in which we might learn about this is to see things as overlapping patchworks of narrative strategies, and Haraway's inspiration in this is the science fiction of Ursula Le Guin, a major figure in the history of twentieth-century environmentalism. The model of the patchwork, the tentative and the exploratory, where we might begin to see the sorts of connections between humankind and other living creatures without recourse to any sort of Spinozist argument about the idea of nature as the ultimate cause of all things, offers more of an explicit politics than some discussions of the 'vibrating matter' of all nature, for example.[24] It still requires us to think about new ways of seeing the earth anew, and uncovering the unspoken assumptions behind ideas about it.

By re-visioning the idea of earth, the global, the planetary, 'home' or 'other', there are obvious ways in which human beings can choose to 'make up' their world, and undertake once more those ways of 'worldmaking' which frame our sense of value. Peoples and personhood are just as much 'made up' through interpretation as anything else, by way of what discussions in historical epistemology suggest are a whole series of tangled loops and connections. The construction of person-relative categories like normal and abnormal or self and other, particularly when we talk about mental illness, has a history that Ian Hacking has delineated in precisely these terms.[25] This making up of new categories and conceptualizations of value was precisely what happened in earlier twentieth-century iterations of this problem, whether in the context of the 'meaning' of Earthrise or debates about a nuclear winter, or when people wrote about *Only One Earth*.[26] Any sense of a shared planet as the location of Anthropocene-time politics needs an awareness of the multiple historical epistemologies that allow us to even talk about its values and categories in the first place.

For critics of singular Anthropocene narratives and epistemologies, like Andreas Malm and Jason Moore, this also requires us to reject the idea of the Anthropocene simply as a result of human agency, and to consider the broader, interlinked structures that buttress the combined and uneven development of modern capitalism in an ecological network connecting all life on the planet. There is no political use, as it were, in blaming 'humanity' for having discovered fire and then used it, but equally there is no 'humanity' that might act as the agent without any conscious capacity, and solve a challenge like the Anthropocene. This is why, despite the fact that most historically minded non-scientific writers on the Anthropocene connect questions of value to questions of capitalism, their examples show that while histories of combined and uneven development have particular path dependencies and pathologies, they are not eternal. The agency behind our politics can change. And the cultivation of a new sort of political agency with a revived conception of ecological value at its heart can readily align with non-Marxist critics of capitalism.[27]

*

Amitav Ghosh, for instance, derives one cause of the 'great derangement' of the Anthropocene from the fact that a certain kind of Western rationality (something he finds to be derived from the 'bourgeois' historical novel and a naturalized fiction about market 'rationality') has been shown up for the myth it always was. But this has happened primarily as a result of major geopolitical shifts across the twentieth century, and of the rise of Asia in particular during the Great Acceleration.[28] In this history, he finds the prospect of an agency that could represent the Anthropocene to result from those traditions of thought and practice that already reject merely 'human' or secular perspectives. That is, in seeking a potentially redemptive subject or agent through which a new politics for the Anthropocene might be formed, Ghosh sees hope in the rejection of secular growth long declared by religious faiths and groups. This comes with its own oddities, though, when a seemingly incongruous cohabitation of Catholicism and conservative environmentalism is back on the agenda today, for example, in Pope Francis's meditation on the legacy of St Francis of Assisi in the papal encyclical *Laudatio Si'* from 2015, or in current protests over fuel tax rises in France that somehow reflect wider right-wing currents of frustration and concern about the limits of national politics, expressed in new journals like *Limite*.[29] Much like Helm's thought that the United States might just turn out to be the future of Anthropocened politics through its own power and advantages, conservative and Christian critics of what they crudely label as fractious and pathological 'identity' politics, for example, unite around a very traditional sense of the environment as something to be shepherded.

However, the conjoined provincializing of Europe presumed by Anthopocene time, the obvious rise in global power of non-European states and regimes, alongside the possibility of rendering the earth itself into a vast sphere of the subaltern, has nevertheless shown certain truths to be self-evident. Economic inequality remains the norm, but the unequal growth that prompted unequal gains in the past cannot continue into the future if, at the very least, current emissions targets are to be met. The obvious injustices of global capitalism during and after the Great Recession merely continue to prove that 'we're all in this together' is little more than discursive, ideological legitimation for continued inequality.[30] Yet because of this conflict, although it promises a great derangement, the Anthropocene remains a moment of political hope. It might provide a sort of historical guide to overcoming the binaries presumed by narratives of a 'clash' of civilizations, in favour of seeing the shared challenges brought about by various crises of civilization.[31] Indeed, there clearly are many different ways in which populations might react to and reject the brazen injustices of their situation, when these are put in historical perspective.

Perhaps the most revealing part of Ghosh's discussion for a political theory of the Anthropocene is how it shows that there are plenty of historical resources for thinking about plural time-frames, spaces and political ideas that have been variously scaled up at different moments, particularly in the wake of specific crises and disasters. Indeed, dealing environmentally with major climate crises and shocks is hardly new, and once again, since the eighteenth century in Europe most obviously, climate science and big data have flourished as human beings have strived to make seemingly 'natural' disasters into 'humanly' explicable issues, subject to critical analyses.[32] Once interpreted, there can be space for political hope while the future remains open, and that future is in principle always open politically, because the politics of the past that frames our sense of the possible is always open to continual reinterpretation. This is one part of the lesson of the modern humanities and social sciences, and which suggests that it is to them, as much as to the natural and physical sciences, that we will have to look for a sense of why we value population, how we might value productivity and life, what we should do to rectify historical injustices, and how we should pluralize the temporalities of our political worlds to avoid the pitfalls of either pessimistic or optimistic fatalism in these new times of the Anthropocene. This, it seems to me, is the real challenge for any sort of realistically Anthropocened politics.

Epilogue
Historical Possibilities for an Anthropocened Politics

It might be true that it remains a 'scandal' that our thinking about politics today has not, despite the wealth of detailed studies we have about how politics functions, got very far in terms of our ability to explain political causality, political possibility and political commitment moving forwards. In part, this is why the history of political thinking retains its contemporary importance for thinking about Anthropocene time. It is not as if reading the works of classic political thinkers will tell us today how to act; rather that some past thinkers, as well as particular moments of historical rupture and transition, remain exemplary in terms of showing us just how complex it is to think about politics across the various dimensions discussed in this book. Past illustrations still show us something about what is required of sophisticated political thinking that tries to combine the historical, the normative and the conceptual, as well as also showing us how political thinking can and often does change through radical acts of conceptual redescription and ideological innovation.[1] If our political challenges are Anthropocened into the widest possible ecological sphere, our political thinking will have to become similarly broadened to accommodate itself to the needs of the moment, and our conceptual narratives will need to evolve. And given that the experience human beings have of the political world is always an historical category, histories of shared forms of lived experience of politics and political thinking will continue to remain instructive into the present. That is the thought I have tried to keep in mind here when connecting debates related to the history of political and economic thought since the 1960s across the terrain of temporality, inequality, growth, population, debts and values, and as these intersect with the similarly shifting terrain of debates about the Anthropocene and its own temporalities, ecologies, presuppositions and perspectives.

Moreover, the Anthropocene is clearly a regime of historicity, a way of seeing a problem or concept across multiple layers of time and space, affected by shifting power dynamics in the political present. In this case, the already complicated layers of political time in the here and now have to contend with the potentially apocalyptic or eschatological time of climate crisis, the deep time of geology, the machine time of artificial intelligence, the accelerated and accelerationist time of the nuclear age, and so on and so forth. This seems to require an awareness of almost impossibly complex and overlapping layers of time that shifts both the Anthropocene and politics into feedback loops of 'backward-looking temporality', but which prohibits the construction of a singular political theory of the Anthropocene. Instead, a properly Anthropocened politics is set against administrative forms of 'solutionism', because neither the Anthropocene, nor politics, is a problem with a solution. Instead, they are shifting predicaments, capable of being argued about and interpreted with reference to shared cultural and political imaginaries, whose limits are contingent, not eternal. The task for politicians and citizens who want to Anthropocene their politics (and thus to make up new political languages) is to try to curate some sense of the scale of what Anthropocene time forces us to confront about political time, and vice versa. For we are the first species we are aware of who are self-conscious of our ecologically transformative pasts that now affect both our present and future and that of the entire earth system.[2]

There's a joke somewhere in the study of the gradually unfreezing Greenland that riffs on the famous concept of flux underwritten by Heraclitus in the origin story of Greek democracy. It has come down to us in Plato's dialogue with the phrase: 'No man ever steps into the same river twice.'

Because the river never stops, and because everything natural is matter in motion, nothing is the same from one moment to the next. Now, though, as the melted ice from the massive glaciers of Greenland flows through the various tributary channels after its frozen sleep across the very deep time of geological chronology, it literally is possible to step into the same river twice. Not exactly laugh out loud funny, but you see the point – thinking about the relationship between time, the Anthropocene, anthropogenic climate change and political action certainly bends our perceptual filters, prompting historicity and complexity as the most prudent response in the face of all the known knowns and unknown knowns of climate catastrophe. That, too, is one of the lessons that the history of political thought offers to contemporary political theory and philosophy, a sort of sceptical awareness of the need to contextualize ideas in their own time in order to trace their continued inscription in the present, because politics and political judgement are not the sorts of things that admit of timeless responses or absolute clarity.

This book has tried to show the resonance and continued relevance of that sceptical way of thinking, in order to cast a rather different light on the challenge of the Anthropocene in the current conjuncture than usually pursued by environmental political theory. Most political theory that considers the Anthropocene through climate ethics tends to focus on those implications which track the three major modes of thinking about climate change – *mitigation*, *adaptation* or *suffering* – offering *technocratic-legalist*, *crisis-response* or *basic adaptability* forms of politics for the modern nation-state in reply.

For example, many philosophers also think climate change poses a real ethical dilemma to human agency, and that it constitutes a 'wicked problem' without singular solutions. Amid the sorts of *technocratic-legalist* readings of modern climate ethics, Stephen Gardiner has provided powerful reasons for rejecting the second claim while retaining the first. In so doing, he shows the weakness of thinking about climate change with reference to human wickedness, or the 'national interest' of states. He focuses instead on why so many of the forms of action that democratic states might plausibly take to curb climate change are politically impossible in practice.[3]

In so doing, Gardiner highlights routine failures of representation in nation-states as the key problem (how many times
do you hear the cry of 'not in my name' as much as 'we're
all in this together'?) in order to suggest that inadequacies
of representation should prompt questions about political
legitimacy. To try to compensate for these failures, something
akin to a constitutional convention for the environment is
often suggested in response, so as to clarify which values
one might want to defend or pursue. This is both a legalistic
solution and a mitigation strategy, where climate change
prompts a rethinking of fundamental ethical values, formal-
izing principles through technical-legal representative bodies.
It adds that the best way to offset problems of action in the
present and into the future is to constitutionalize procedures
now, but for the future, which is epistemically justified
with reference to certain principles in modern democratic
theory (such as forms of epistocratic rule by experts, or the
continued adherence to free and fair elections across fixed
periods). That might entrench the democratic presumption
that there is always the potential to change your mind when
the facts change, while also registering the fact that our
own moral values and intuitions based around them are of
relatively recent vintage, and certainly not eternal. If, as Dale
Jamieson argues, our 'modern' sensibilities arose late and
in low-population-density and low-technology societies, as
those conditions change and many democracies transition
into demographically aged, technologically advanced,
extremely prosperous places, so too can values transition.[4] In
both senses, we are able to free ourselves to think about the
moral demands both past and future generations place on us
from within Anthropocene time.

In this vein, many works on environmental political theory
and climate justice also analyse the reciprocal relationship
between human and natural agency. For some, therefore, a
related kind of 'constitutional environmentalism' might be
grounded on a fundamental shared interest in the 'integrity'
of the relationship between human beings and the natural
world. This is not quite the same as upholding any kind
of 'intrinsic value' in nature that human beings should
worship or valorize.[5] For others still, a better bet is a sort of
'ecocentric' philosophy that promotes a virtue of 'humility'

(or even indifference, which again is a form of toleration) in dealing with nature. That would suggest we require neither a radically eco-socialist nor a conservatively minded focus on stewardship, but something which reconfigures the relationship between human agency and the natural world as one of participation and mutual care.[6]

Writers who are more interested in the ethical and justice-related implications of climate change also often suggest that the unevenly distributed burdens of climate change, which disadvantage the already disadvantaged most directly, could be rectified if it was thought about as a problem of human rights. Instead of an 'economic' route of discounting, the 'philosophical' route of dissolving the distance between past and future for moral purposes, or the 'security' dilemmas around energy, food and land (which governmental agencies see as the principal exponential 'threat' posed by climate change), human rights might offer a basis for thinking about international and inter-generational justice. It seems likely that the blunt forces of geopolitics and food security will be more immediately compelling drivers of nation-state policy in the immediate term, with human rights a co-benefit of such strategies at best. But this is why the challenge of how we can incorporate the Anthropocene into the political realm matters so much for a shared political future, based on an appraisal of how politics has come to be formed in and through the modern state and its critics.[7]

Human rights arguments seek their justification on grounds that respect human flourishing, and these can guarantee rights by compelling duties on the part of agents who engage in climate-altering actions. This is also a space where non-human entities and substances can be granted rights by means of similar legal fictions to those which give artificial life to corporations and states, and which in turn might direct action such as taxing polluters or excessive carbon emitters in more conventional ways. 'Basic rights' within the human rights canon – rights to health, life and subsistence – are upheld by human and artificial or fictive corporate agents and states not only on behalf of other human beings, but also potentially on behalf of forms of natural life. Even though the idea of 'basic rights', at first at least, was part of a discourse about what American foreign policy might be able to achieve in the 1970s and involved figures like Robert McNamara at the World Bank, these rights could in principle travel widely.[8] They might provide another sort of background condition of 'realistic utopia', one that can offer a regulative ideal to hope for and work towards. But without hard political choices to maintain and increase standards of economic and social welfare, such human or basic rights models will remain an area subject to considerable scepticism, one where much suffering is amply recognized, but about which not very much is practically done. What else, then, beyond a sort of chastened scepticism and plea for political prudence in Anthropocene time, is there to learn from the history of political and economic thought?

First, a reminder that modern politics in a representative mode is, among other things, a regime designed to distribute and share economic and political risks collectively, under conditions of quite radical epistemic uncertainty. It is unequal, and uneven, of course, but there is a big-picture claim from the eighteenth-century origin story that holds true now. The evolution of global commerce, theorized so extensively then, posed the question of whether or not commercial competition was likely to lead to peace through profit, or jealousy of trade that would lead to war by other means. In many ways, that remains the key question of modern economic and political competition on the international stage. And if global dynamics of war and peace relate to economic competition, they also relate to the Anthropocene. For both, how we choose to distribute the myriad risks of action and inaction into an open future, while recognizing the tangled relations involved in such considerations, frames the extent of the challenge.

It seems very unlikely that domestic autarky is a viable response to these challenges, which suggests that domestic politics and politicians can best begin to tackle the issues by honestly engaging with their electorates about the options that are open to them. It will also mean paying a pretty steep price if the first step towards Anthropocened politics is mitigating the negative effects of climate change. Within this, scholars, scientists, experts and publics all have a responsibility to do what they can, and experts in political thought and intellectual history can at the very least try to think through the implications of what a truly global approach to their subject will require if it is to tackle a truly global challenge.[9] In tandem with this, an Anthropocened politics must work to rethink the state theory upon which it is routinely premised, to highlight the ways in which 'being ecological' can become part of the norm of a strategic and relational approach to governance and government.[10] Furthermore, when thinking about what sorts of metamorphoses might be required of citizens making Anthropocene-time-relevant political choices, compensating for misalignments in the distribution of resources is only a partial step. Instead, as Elizabeth Anderson has long suggested, more radically democratic and relational forms of equality that can adapt to the shifting values of egalitarian societies seem a much more promising foundation upon which political philosophy can contribute to debates around climate change and its effects.[11]

Second, if the future is not to be foreclosed (at least in part because the challenge of the Anthropocene proves to us once again that pure fatalism really is a fool's errand in politics), then we might want to consider strategies for planning more coordinated international responses. This is more speculative, but in that vein, and learning the lessons from nuclear strategy for present threats, some of those who think about cyberwarfare have suggested that defensive mobilization is a more likely and historically proven option to bring states together to coordinate responses, rather than seeking to go on the offensive with dramatic new directions led by hegemonic powers. Though it remains difficult to see how such associations could avoid becoming tools of the already powerful, the sorts of conventions on defensive cyberwarfare strategy that have been proposed might also become models for thinking about defensive political-time strategies for dealing with Anthropocene time.[12] It might also provide a way for beginning to think about how the politics of the Anthropocene can be combined with the science of climate change overseen through institutions like the IPCC in new forms of functional internationalism. Similarly, a federalized international body, embodying experts and elected citizens and representing every country on the planet, funded by a dedicated amalgamation of sovereign wealth funds, paid for in part through the preliminary rectification of historical injustices and ecological debts on the part of the global North, may sound little more than wildly utopian. It, too, however, could offer new sites within which to discuss international politics in the age of the Anthropocene, outside of the confines of existing institutional structures and their entrenched narratives.

Where such considerations as, say, a capital levy were discussed as options for dealing in an inter-generationally just way with the problem of indebtedness and reconstruction after the First World War by welfare economists like Pigou, now we might need to revisit another aspect of those connections. As already suggested by many others, we might have to take seriously the thought that the challenge of the Anthropocene for modern politics is to see it as akin to a war being fought for the survival of planet Earth. This is where the focus of alternative responses to a politics of the Anthropocene, whether democratic or authoritarian, might develop. These could run the gamut from global constitutionalism to constitutional dictatorship on the model of a war economy, entrenching norms and values that can survive an enemy that cannot be defeated on any conventional or post-conventional battlefield. Call this the *crisis-response* paradigm, where the response to the Anthropocene is to engage in a war for the earth. In Latour's rendering, this will be a conflict between 'modern' human beings and 'terrestrials', one amplified by the daily round of polemical warfare between democracy and truth, as exemplified by the current occupant of the White House.[13]

Equally, however, it might just be the continuation of democratic politics by other means. After all, political scientists have long thought of minimal sorts of representative democratic system, such as those that exist in large parts of the world, as proxies for war. The sense of their having a 'value' beyond the merely procedural accrues over time in that those countries who have adopted minimal systems of democratic and electoral competition tend to have become those countries who longer engage in actual military conflict with one another. Pressing the analogy still further, if the battle for the Anthropocene is really a battle for control of the intellectual horizons of modern politics, then it might be useful to consider the challenge one of mobilizing resources and ideas, seeing new ways of understanding our shared future and providing possible forms of leadership. For Latour, once more, this might require thinking beyond capitalism, cultivating new 'critical spaces' that might act as both moral and political exemplars for a new future. In his own accounting, Europe, for all its historical flaws and colonial lineages, might nevertheless signal the possibility of a post-national and federational union of states, capable of being a sort of moral beacon to the world, a renewed 'friend of humanity'.[14]

At one level, this is also analogous to the sort of 'constitutional patriotism' envisaged by Jürgen Habermas, where previously emotional attachments to nations and nationalism might be progressively subverted in favour of a more rational and enlightened commitment to the parameters of a constitution, as illustrated, in his mind, by the evolution of Europe.[15] Can European states today play such roles? Well, to me this is actually to come late to the party, and in similar ways that the political origins of debates about global justice in Western political theory followed late to a party that had already begun in the anti-colonial and post-colonial politics that shaped the contours of a post-First World War world outside of America and old Europe. As critiques of the imperial dynamics of the nation-state continued until the period of decolonization, the Bandung Conference and then into proposals for a New International Economic Order, there is a long and rich legacy of thinking about how to connect post-imperial federations with an anti-capitalist focus based around shared values. If the Anthropocene challenges us to see the connections between capitalism, colonialism and economic value, on the one hand, and the alternative possibilities to them, on the other, we could surely do worse than work to recover the still-often occluded histories of anti-colonial political thought into the wider mainstream of public discussion.

Third, and following this train of thought, one suggestion for how to reconnect with a much wider, more intellectually open and broader-gauge approach to the new times of the Anthropocene is to go back to older traditions of political economy and welfare economics that were operative when it was part of a general science of moral reasoning. This might become a sort of *basic-adaptability* paradigm. Maybe we can learn to adapt from earlier debates about financing, taxation and capital levies that were discussed when it came to thinking of post-war reconstruction in ways that understood the complexities of inter-generational and international justice. Again, if Anthropocene time really is war by other means, then figuring out how to pay for how that war was caused and for its consequences requires some new and creative thinking about the relationships between state power, economic growth, ecological indebtedness and historical injustice. It will also require the production of new forms of accountancy and management, ones that can incorporate more fine-grained analyses of human as well as more broadly ecological measurements of well-being than can conventional metrics of GDP.

This would be an optimistic rendering of the basic-adaptability paradigm, one where, for example, a principled commitment to divestment, on the one hand, and the promulgation of something like a Green New Deal, on the other, could be practical and attractive policy positions for politicians and citizens willing to try to reorient the mainstream narratives. But it is important not to get the causal claims the wrong way around. Many seem to think that climate change is dangerous because it leads to conflict, and that's why it needs to be controlled. But as historical geographers have long noted, climatic determinism and reductionism has a long history of political simplification, suggesting that life is fated to go one way rather than another.[16] Following that route absolves us of any political responsibility to think about how to act in the face of climate change, and leaves the field open to those who would pursue that thought and then weaponize nature itself in response, as military thinking about swarms and artificial intelligence has been doing for some time already.[17]

A properly Anthropocened politics will be compelled to think harder about these relationships in order to keep options open and not succumb to the easy pessimism that politics cannot go beyond the conventional nostrums of national political-economic management in a world controlled by high finance capital. Indeed, a deeply Anthropocened politics must eventually serve to remind us that political choices are complex decisions about the past, present and future; they take place across many different axes and involve many representational claims. This can also serve to remind us that we need never simply be beholden to something so fickle or so fixed as 'fate' when thinking about politics and political time, even political time in the new world of Anthropocene time. That might sound wildly optimistic, utopian even, but it is certainly not a glib thought. If representative politics is to do more than merely survive or just settle for adaptation, it must meet the challenge of the Anthropocene by embracing its complexity, rethinking its pasts and imagining new futures based on shared historical experience. This requires an ongoing challenge to the established narratives of a liberal world order, which to my mind remains the most realistic future for representative political thinking to pursue into the new times of the Anthropocene.

Notes

Prologue: The New Political Times of the Anthropocene

1 Simon Lewis and Mark Maslin, *The Human Planet: How We Created the Anthropocene* (London, 2018), p. 237.
2 Paul Crutzen and Eugene Stoermer, 'The Anthropocene', *Global Change Newsletter* 41 (2000), pp. 17–18.
3 Paul Crutzen, John Birks and J. W. Heinrichsen (eds), *The Atmosphere after a Nuclear War: Twilight at Noon* (Oxford, 1982); cf. 'Paul Crutzen on the Ozone Hole, Nitrogen Oxides, and the Nobel Prize', *Angewandte* 52.1 (2013), pp. 48–50.
4 Jeremy Davies, *The Birth of the Anthropocene* (Berkeley, CA, 2006), p. 15.
5 Erle Ellis, *The Anthropocene: A Very Short Introduction* (Oxford, 2018), p. 130.
6 Katrina Forrester and Sophie Smith (eds), *Nature, Action and the Future* (Cambridge, 2018).
7 See William Cronon, 'The Trouble with Wilderness: Or, Getting Back to the Wrong Nature', *Environmental History* 1.1 (1996), pp. 7–28.
8 John Maynard Keynes, *The General Theory of Employment, Interest and Money* (London, 1936).
9 For Nelson Goodman, *Ways of Worldmaking* (Indianapolis, 1972), this is simply because we can only ever interpret the world through the conceptual schemes we develop to make sense of what we think is important. Cf. Duncan Bell, 'Making and Taking Worlds', in S. Moyn and A. Sartori (eds), *Global*

Intellectual History (Ithaca, NY, 2013), pp. 254–80. For one recent use of the concept of 'generation' to make sense of the worldmaking of revolutionary politics, see Roy Foster, *Vivid Faces: The Revolutionary Generation in Ireland, 1890–1922* (London, 2014).

10 For two general histories, see Peter Coates, *Nature* (Oxford, 1998), esp. pp. 108, 174f., 190f.; and Joachim Radkau, *Nature and Power* (Cambridge, 2008).

11 Cf. Niall Ferguson, Charles S. Maier, Erez Manela and Daniel J. Sargent (eds), *The Shock of the Global: The 1970s in Perspective* (Cambridge, MA, 2010).

12 Cf. Jedediah Purdy, *After Nature* (Cambridge, MA, 2016); and 'Environmentalism's Racist History', *New Yorker* (13 August 2015): https://www.newyorker.com/news/news-desk/environmentalisms-racist-history.

13 Katrina Forrester, 'The Anthropocene Truism', *The Nation* (12 May 2016).

14 Alison Bashford, 'The Anthropocene is Modern History: Reflections on Climate and Australian Deep Time', *Australian Historical Studies* 44.3 (2013), pp. 341–9; and Andrew Fitzmaurice, 'The Genealogy of *Terra Nullius*', *Australian Historical Studies* 39.3 (2008), pp. 1–15.

Chapter 1 Timings

1 Michael Drolet, 'Nature, Science and the Environment in Nineteenth-Century French Political Economy: The Case of Michel Chevalier', *Modern Intellectual History* 15.3 (2018), pp. 711–45; Sverker Sörlin and Paul Warde (eds), *Nature's End: History and the Environment* (Basingstoke, 2009); and Paul Warde, *The Invention of Sustainability: Nature, Human Action and Destiny, 1500–1870* (Cambridge, 2018). For political theory, the major eighteenth-century text to theorize a relationship between climate and constitutionalism is Montesquieu, *The Spirit of the Laws*, ed. and trans A. Cohler (Cambridge, 1988).

2 Serge Audier, *La société écologique et ses ennemis* (Paris, 2017).

3 The Royal Society, *Geo-engineering the Climate* (London, 2009), p. 11.

4 William B. Meyer, 'Edward Bellamy and the Weather of Utopia', *The Geographical Review* 94.1 (2004), pp. 43–54.

5 See Eglė Rindzevičiūtė, 'Soviet Policy Sciences and Earth System Governmentality', *Modern Intellectual History* (2018), pp. 1–30: https://doi.org/10.1017/S1479244318000161.

6 Ibid., p. 15.
7 Paul Crutzen, 'Geology of Mankind', *Nature* 415.3 (2002), p. 23.
8 For wider context, see Martin Rudwick, *Earth's Deep History* (Chicago, 2014).
9 Crutzen and Stoermer, 'The Anthropocene'; for wider discussion, see See Andreas Malm, *Fossil Capital* (London, 2014).
10 The 'golden spike' is shorthand for the location of an internationally agreed-upon stratigraphic section, or 'Global Boundary Stratotype Section Point' (GSSP).
11 E. A. Wrigley, *Energy and the Industrial Revolution* (Cambridge, 2010); and, more recently, his *The Path to Sustained Growth: England's Transition from an Organic Economy to an Industrial Revolution* (Cambridge, 2016).
12 Daron Acemoglu and James Robinson, *Why Nations Fail: The Origins of Power, Prosperity and Poverty* (London, 2013).
13 Thad Dunning, *Crude Democracy* (Cambridge, 2008).
14 Dieter Helm, *Burnout: The Endgame for Fossil Fuels* (New Haven, CT, 2018); and James Barr, *Lords of the Desert: Britain's Struggle with America to Dominate the Middle East* (London, 2018).
15 Timothy Mitchell, *Carbon Democracy* (London, 2013); cf. his *Rule of Experts: Egypt, Techno-Politics, Modernity* (Berkeley, CA, 2002).
16 Acemoglu and Robinson, *Why Nations Fail*, pp. 437–43.
17 Adam Przeworski, *Democracy and the Limits to Self-Government* (Cambridge, 2011); and John Dunn, *Setting the People Free* (London, 2006).
18 The lawyer and legal historian Frederic W. Maitland made this point clear in a sparkling and very complex series of essays about legal personality and corporate identity which have been hugely influential for modern political theory. See F. W. Maitland, *Political Writings*, eds D. Runciman and M. Ryan (Cambridge, 2005).
19 Benjamin Constant, 'The Liberty of the Ancients Compared to that of the Moderns', *Constant – Political Writings*, ed. B. Fontana (Cambridge, 1988), pp. 308–28.
20 Martin Gilens, *Affluence and Influence* (Princeton, NJ, 2014); Martin Gilens and Benjamin Page, 'Testing Theories of American Politics: Elites, Interest Groups and Average Citizens', *Perspectives on Politics* 12.3 (2014), pp. 564–81; and David Runciman, *How Democracy Ends* (London, 2018).
21 Cf. Nadia Urbinati, *Genealogy of Representative Government* (Chicago, 2006); and *Democracy Disfigured* (Cambridge, MA,

2016). On the moral dimensions of this temporal disconnect for street-level bureaucrats, see Bernardo Zacka, *Where the State Meets the Street* (Cambridge, MA, 2017).

22 Max Weber, 'The Profession and Vocation of Politics', in *Weber: Political Writings*, ed. P. Lassman and R. Speirs (Cambridge, 1994), pp. 309–69, p. 369.

23 Bill McKibben, 'A Very Grim Forecast', *New York Review of Books* (22 November 2018); and 'How Extreme Weather is Shrinking the Planet', *New Yorker* (26 November 2018): https://www.newyorker.com/magazine/2018/11/26/how-extreme-weather-is-shrinking-the-planet. See too IPCC Report, 2018, *Global Warming of 1.5°C*: https://www.ipcc.ch/sr15/.

24 See David Runciman, *The Confidence Trap* (Princeton, NJ, 2018).

25 Simon Lewis, 'Don't Despair – Climate Change Catastrophe Can Still Be Averted', *The Guardian* (7 August 2018): https://www.theguardian.com/commentisfree/2018/aug/07/climate-change-catastrophe-political-will-grassroots-engagement.

26 François Hartog, *Regimes of Historicity*, trans. S. Brown (New York, 2017).

27 Marcia Bjornerud, *Timefulness: How Thinking Like a Geologist Can Help Save the World* (Princeton, NJ, 2018); and Lewis and Maslin, *Human Planet*, pp. 29, 121f., 143, 279ff.

28 Michael Hulme, *Why We Disagree About Climate Change* (Cambridge, 2009), pp. 325, 329, 331, 341.

29 Reinhart Koselleck, *Futures Past*, trans. K. Tribe (New York, 2000).

30 See Mark Salber Philips, 'Rethinking Historical Distance: From Doctrine to Heuristic', *History and Theory* 50 (2011), pp. 11–23.

31 World Commission on Environment and Development (WCED), *Our Common Future* (Oxford, 1987), p. 43.

32 Karl Polanyi, *The Great Transformation* (Boston, 2001).

33 W. E. B. Du Bois, 'World War and the Color Line', *The Crisis* 9.1 (1914), pp. 28–30; 'The African Roots of the War', *Atlantic Monthly* (May 1915), pp. 707–14; and 'Close Ranks', *The Crisis* 16.3 (1918), pp. 111–14. Mohandas Gandhi, *Hind Swaraj*, ed. A. J. Parel (Cambridge, 2010). Cf. Pankaj Mishra, 'How Colonial Violence Came Home: The Ugly Truth of the First World War', *The Guardian* (10 November 2017): https://www.theguardian.com/news/2017/nov/10/how-colonial-violence-came-home-the-ugly-truth-of-the-first-world-war.

34 Frantz Fanon, *The Wretched of the Earth*, trans. C. Farrington (London, 2001), p. 27.

35 Jill Lepore, 'The Atomic Origins of Climate Science', *New Yorker* (30 January 2017): https://www.newyorker.com/ magazine/2017/01/30/the-atomic-origins-of-climate-science; her essay popularizes Matthias Dörries, 'The Politics of Atmospheric Science: "Nuclear Winter" and Global Climate Change', *Osiris* 26 (2011), pp. 198–223; cf. Radkau, *Nature and Power*, pp. 239–49.

36 Cf. Sonja Amadae, *Rationalizing Capitalist Democracy* (Chicago, 2003); and *Prisoners of Reason* (Cambridge, 2015).

37 Barry Katz, 'The Frankfurt School Goes to War', *Journal of Modern History* 59.3 (1987), pp. 439–78; and Franz Neumann, Herbert Marcuse and Otto Kirchheimer, *Secret Reports on Nazi Germany*, ed. R. Laudani, (Princeton, NJ, 2013).

38 On the historical novelty of such ways of thinking about cooperation between individuals and between states, cf. Richard Tuck, *Free Riding* (Cambridge, MA, 2008); and Thomas Schelling, *The Strategy of Conflict* (Cambridge, MA, 1960).

39 Cf. John Dunn, 'Political Obligations and Political Possibilities', in *Political Obligation in Its Historical Context* (Cambridge, 1979), pp. 243–300; and Martin Hollis, *Models of Man* (Cambridge, 1977).

40 Albert Hirschmann, *The Rhetoric of Reaction* (Cambridge, MA, 1999).

41 Cf. Joel Isaac, 'Strategy as Intellectual History', *Modern Intellectual History* (2018): https://doi.org/10.1017/ S1479244318000094.

42 See Adam Shatz, 'The President and the Bomb', *London Review of Books* (16 November 2017).

43 Project Sunshine, *Worldwide Effects of Atomic Weapons* (RAND, 1953); on Wexler, see James Fleming, 'Weather and Climate as Shape-Shifting Nouns: Gordian Knots of Understanding and Prevision', *History of Meteorology* 7 (2015), pp. 1–13, at pp. 10–12.

44 Joel Isaac, *Working Knowledge* (Cambridge, MA, 2012); and Ira Katznelson, *Desolation and Enlightenment* (New York, 2005).

45 John von Neumann, 'Can We Survive Technology?' *Fortune* (1955 repr.): http://fortune.com/2013/01/13/can-we-survive-technology/ .

46 Dörries, 'Atmospheric Science', pp. 218f.; cf. Paul Crutzen and John Birks, 'The Atmosphere After a Nuclear War: Twilight at Noon', *Ambio* 11.2/3 (1982), pp. 114–25; Paul Ehrlich and Carl Sagan, *The Cold and the Dark: The World After Nuclear War* (New York, 1984).

47 Quinn Slobodian, *Globalists* (Cambridge, MA, 2018).

48 See Paul Warde (with Sverker Sörlin), 'Expertise for the Future: The Emergence of "Relevant Knowledge" in Environmental Predictions and Global Change, c.1920–1970', in Jenny Andersson and Eglė Rindzevičiūtė (eds), *The Struggle for the Long-Term in Transnational Science and Politics During the Cold War* (Abingdon, 2015), pp. 39–62, esp. pp. 42ff. The original book is William Vogt, *The Road to Survival* (London, 1948).

49 Clinton Rossiter, 'Constitutional Dictatorship in the Atomic Age', *The Review of Politics* 11.4 (1949), pp. 395–418; cf. Martin Rees, *On the Future: Prospects for Humanity* (Princeton, NJ, 2018).

50 See Rebecca Altman, 'Time Bombing the Future: How 20th Century Synthetics Altered the Fabric of Us All', *Aeon*: https://aeon.co/essays/how-20th-century-synthetics-altered-the-very-fabric-of-us-all.

51 IPCC Report, 2018, pp. 41, 26, 31.

52 Ibid., pp. 10 and 31; cf. Fiona Harvey, '"Tipping Points" Could Exacerbate Climate Change, Scientists Fear', *The Guardian*, 9 October 2018: https://www.theguardian.com/environment/2018/oct/09/tipping-points-could-exacerbate-climate-crisis-scientists-fear; and Damian Carrington, 'Humanity Has Wiped Out 60% of Animal Populations since 1970, Report Finds', *The Guardian*, 30 October 2018: https://www.theguardian.com/environment/2018/oct/30/humanity-wiped-out-animals-since-1970-major-report-finds.

53 Stephen F. Foley et al., 'The Paleoanthropocene – The Beginnings of Anthropogenic Environmental Change', *Anthropocene* 3 (2013), pp. 83–8.

54 Cf. Daniel Lord Smail, *Deep History and the Brain* (Berkeley, CA, 2008).

55 Dipesh Chakrabarty, 'Anthropocene Time', *History and Theory* 57.1 (2018), pp. 5–32.

56 Martin Mahoney and Mike Hulme, 'Epistemic Geographies of Climate Change: Science, Space and Politics', *Progress in Human Geography* 42.3 (2018), pp. 395–424; in general terms, Radkau, *Nature and Power*, ch. 5; cf. Kathryn Yusoff, *A Billion Black Anthropocenes or None* (Minneapolis, MN, 2018)

57 For different reflections on the non-novelty of the Anthropocene, see Geoffrey Parker, *Global Crisis: War, Climate Change and Catastrophe in the Seventeenth Century* (New Haven, CT, 2013); Christophe Bonneuil and Jean-Baptiste Fressoz, *The Shock of the Anthropocene* (London, 2017); Audier, *La société écologique*; Ellis, *Anthropocene*; Lewis and Maslin, *Human Planet*, pp. 23, 29.

58 I borrow this phrase from Troy Vettesse, 'Climate Gut Check', *Boston Review*, 5 December 2018: http://bostonreview.net/ science-nature/troy-vettese-climate-gut-check.

59 Bill McKibben, 'At Last, Divestment Is Hitting the Fossil Fuel Industry Where It Hurts', *The Guardian*, 16 December 2018: https://www.theguardian.com/commentisfree/2018/dec/16/ divestment-fossil-fuel-industry-trillions-dollars-investments-carbon.

60 See Deborah Coen, 'Big is a Thing of the Past: Climate Change and Methodology in the History of Ideas', *Journal of the History of Ideas* 77.2 (2016), pp. 305–21.

61 Warde (with Sörlin), 'Expertise for the Future'.

Chapter 2 Ecological Inequalities

1 Slobodian, *Globalists*, p. 281. Cf. John O'Neil and Thomas Uebel, 'Between Frankfurt and Vienna: Two Traditions of Political Ecology', in Forrester and Smith (eds), *Nature, Action and the Future*, pp. 133–56.

2 Eden Medina, *Cybernetic Revolutionaries: Technology and Politics in Allende's Chile* (Cambridge, MA, 2014); and Evgeny Morysov, 'The Socialist Origins of Big Data', *New Yorker* (13 October 2014): https://www.newyorker. com/magazine/2014/10/13/planning-machine. Cf. Naomi Klein, *The Shock Doctrine* (London, 2008). Images of the operation room are here: https://99percentinvisible.org/episode/ project-cybersyn/.

3 Bob Jessop, *The State* (Oxford, 2015).

4 Warde (with Sörlin), 'Expertise for the Future'.

5 Simon Kuznets, 'Economic Growth and Income Inequality', *American Economic Review* 45.1 (1955), pp. 1–28.

6 Danny Dorling, *Do We Need Economic Inequality?* (Oxford, 2018), pp. 17, 25.

7 Naomi Klein, *This Changes Everything* (London, 2015).

8 Cf. Michel Foucault, *The Order of Things* (London, 2001); Adam Tooze, *Statistics and the German State* (Cambridge, 2001); and Donald Mackenzie, *An Engine, not a Camera: How Financial Models Shape Markets* (Cambridge, MA, 2008).

9 Friedrich Nietzsche, *On the Genealogy of Morality*, ed. Keith Ansell-Pearson (Cambridge, 1998).

10 Timothy Morton, *Being Ecological* (London, 2018), p. 63.

11 Ibid., p. 177.

12 Cf. Robert Macfarlane, 'Generation Anthropocene: How

Humans Have Altered the Planet For Ever', *The Guardian* (1 April 2016): https://www.theguardian.com/books/2016/apr/01/generation-anthropocene-altered-planet-for-ever.

13 Morton, *Being Ecological*, pp. 198f, 201, 208ff., 213f.

14 Cf. Helen Thompson, *Oil and the Western Economic Crisis* (Basingstoke, 2017).

15 Kate Raworth, *Doughnut Economics* (New York, 2018).

16 Rachel Carson, 'Silent Spring, Part I', *New Yorker* (16 June 1962): https://www.newyorker.com/magazine/1962/06/16/silent-spring-part-1; 'Silent Spring, Part II', *New Yorker* (23 June 1962): https://www.newyorker.com/magazine/1962/06/23/silent-spring-part-2; and 'Silent Spring, Part III', *New Yorker* (30 June 1962): https://www.newyorker.com/magazine/1962/06/30/silent-spring-part-3.

17 David Pearce, 'An Intellectual History of Environmental Economics', *Annual Review of Energy and the Environment* 27 (2002), pp. 57–81, at pp. 57f. Cf. Ian Kumekawa, *The First Serious Optimist* (Cambridge, MA, 2017), which considers the work of Arthur Pigou, one of the pioneering figures in modern welfare economics and the intellectual progenitor of the 'polluter pays' principle, and outlines the intellectual contexts in which he developed his ideas.

18 Pearce, 'Intellectual History', p. 75; cf. Mark Sagoff, 'The Rise and Fall of Ecological Economics', *Breakthrough Journal* 2 (2011): https://thebreakthrough.org/journal/issue-2/the-rise-and-fall-of-ecological-economics.

19 Joan Martinez-Alier, *Ecological Economics* (London, 1987).

20 Max Weber, '"Energetical" Theories of Culture' [1909], in *Collected Methodological Writings*, trans. H. H. Bruun, eds H. H. Bruun and S. Whimster (London, 2012), pp. 252–68.

21 John Bellamy Foster, 'Weber and the Environment: Classical Foundations for a Postexemptionist Sociology', *American Journal of Sociology* 117.6 (2012), pp. 1625–73.

22 Max Weber, 'Die wirtschaftliche Zugehörigkeit des Saargebiets zu Deutschland', in *Zur Neuordnung Deutschlands, Max Weber Gesamtausgabe* 1/16, ed. W, Mommsen (Tübingen, 1988), pp. 236f, 239.

23 Martinez-Alier, *Ecological Economics*, p. 183; and Shellen Xiao Wu, *Empires of Coal* (New York, 2015), p. 189.

24 Cf. Richard Tuck, 'The Contribution of History', in Robert E. Goodin and Philip Pettit (eds), *A Companion to Contemporary Political Philosophy* (Oxford, 1991), pp. 72–89.

25 W. S. Jevons, *The Coal Question* (London, 1865); for the wider connections in Tory and Christian political economy

to geology, see Boyd Hilton, *The Age of Atonement* (Oxford, 1996).

26 See Fredrik Albritton-Jonsson, 'Political Economy', in Mark Bevir (ed.), *Historicism and the Human Sciences in Victorian England* (Cambridge, 2017), pp. 186–210; and 'The Coal Question before Jevons', *Historical Journal* (2019): https://doi.org/10.1017/S0018246X19000153; cf. Nuno Luis Madureira, 'The Anxiety of Abundance: William Stanley Jevons and Coal Scarcity in the Nineteenth Century', *Environment and History* 18 (2012), pp. 395–421.

27 Christopher Otter 'Liberty and Ecology: Resources, Markets and the British Contribution to the Global Environmental Crisis', in James Vernon and Simon Gunn (eds), *Peculiarities of Liberal Modernity in Imperial Britain* (Manchester, 2011), pp. 182–98.

28 For twentieth-century iterations of this, see Alison Bashford, *Global Population* (Ithaca, NY, 2015).

29 Jevons, *The Coal Question*, p. 349.

30 Daniel Yergin, *The Quest: Energy, Security and the Remaking of the Modern World* (New York, 2011).

31 For the imperial nostalgia behind the Anglosphere, see Duncan Bell, 'The Anglosphere: New Enthusiasm for an Old Dream', *Prospect* (19 January 2017): https://www.prospectmagazine.co.uk/magazine/anglosphere-old-dream-brexit-role-in-the-world.

32 Thompson, *Oil*, p. 99.

33 William James, 'Proposing the Moral Equivalent of War', lecture at Stanford University, 1906: https://www.laphamsquarterly.org/states-war/proposing-moral-equivalent-war.

34 Thompson, *Oil*, pp. 103ff.; and Helm, *Burnout*.

35 Branko Milanovic, *Global Inequality* (Cambridge, MA, 2018), chs 1–3.

36 For different but related concerns, see Jim Bulpitt, 'The Discipline of the New Democracy: Mrs Thatcher's Domestic Statecraft', *Political Studies* 34.1 (1986), pp. 19–39; and Helen Thompson, 'Inevitability and Contingency: The Political Economy of Brexit', *British Journal of Politics and International Relations* 19.3 (2017), pp. 434–49.

37 Kuznets, 'Economic Growth', p. 10.

38 Ibid., p. 16.

39 Ibid., p. 28.

40 Thomas Piketty, *Capital in the Twenty-First Century*, trans. A. Goldhammer (Cambridge, MA, 2015), pp. 149, 204f., 233, 402.

41 Walter Scheidel, *The Great Leveller* (Princeton, NJ, 2016); Simon Reid Henry, *The Political Origins of Inequality* (Chicago, 2015); and Adam Przeworski, 'Minimalist Conception of Democracy:

A Defence', in Ian Shapiro and Casiano Hacker-Cordón (eds), *Democracy's Value* (Cambridge, 2001), pp. 23–55.

42 Göran Therborn, *Cities of Power* (London, 2017); and Edward Luce, *The Crisis of Western Liberalism* (London, 2017). For a classic recent discussion, Mike Davis, *City of Quartz* (New York, 1998).

43 Ulrich Beck, *The Metamorphosis of the World* (Oxford, 2016), pp. 179ff.

44 Ash Amin and Nigel Thrift, *Seeing like a City* (Oxford, 2016).

45 Ashley Dawson, *Extreme Cities* (London, 2017).

46 Cf. Piketty, *Capital*, pp. 234, 334f.

47 Peter H. Lindert and Jeffrey G. Williamson, *Unequal Gains: American Growth and Inequality since 1700* (Princeton, NJ, 2016), pp. 194ff.

48 Ibid., pp. 203, 215–18.

49 Ibid., pp. 220ff.

Chapter 3 Limiting Growth?

1 Dipesh Chakrabarty, 'Climate and Capital: Conjoined Histories', *Critical Inquiry* 41 (2014), pp. 1–23, at p. 1. The original idea of a metabolic rift between humanity and nature derives from Marx.

2 Laura Díaz Anadón, Erin Baker and Valentina Bosetti, 'Integrating Uncertainty into Public Energy Research and Development Decisions', *Nature/Energy* 2 (2017), p. 1: DOI: 10.1038/nenergy.2017.71   https://www.nature.com/articles/nenergy201771?proof=true

3 Michelle Brattain, 'Race, Racism, and Antiracism: UNESCO and the Politics of Presenting Science to the Post-War Public', *American Historical Review* 112.5 (2007), pp. 1386–413, documents another instance of the interconnection between race, science and politics in the formation of international institutions.

4 Chakrabarty, 'Climate and Capital', p. 9.

5 Thomas Meaney, 'A Celebrity Philosopher Explains the Populist Insurgency', *New Yorker* (26 February 2018): https://www.newyorker.com/magazine/2018/02/26/a-celebrity-philosopher-explains-the-populist-insurgency.

6 On the terminology, see Matthias Dörries, 'Climate Catastrophes and Fear', *Climate Change* 1 (2010), pp. 885–90.

7 Cf. Runciman, *How Democracy Ends*; and Steven Levitsky and Daniel Ziblatt, *How Democracies Die* (London, 2017).

8 On the British case, Peter Sloman, 'Redistribution in an Age of Neoliberalism', *Political Studies* (2018): https://doi.org/10.1177/0032321718800495. On the broader political theory of decolonization and self-determination, Adom Getachew, *Worldmaking After Empire: The Rise and Fall of Self-Determination* (Princeton, NJ, 2019).

9 Cf. Jürgen Habermas, *The Lure of Technocracy*, trans. C. Cronin (Oxford, 2015); and 'Conservatism and Capitalist Crisis', *New Left Review* I/115 (1979), pp. 73–86. Charles Maier, '"Malaise": The Crisis of Capitalism in the 1970s', in Ferguson et al. (eds), *Shock of the Global*, pp. 25–48.

10 R. John Williams, *The Buddha in the Machine* (New Haven, CT, 2014).

11 For an interesting account of Drucker, see Ian F. McNeely, 'Peter Drucker's Protestant Ethic', *Modern Intellectual History* (2018): https://doi.org/10.1017/S1479244318000525; cf. Linda Weiss, *The Myth of the Powerless State* (Oxford, 1998), for a critique of the sort of hyper-globalization thesis once espoused by Ohmae.

12 Wolfgang Streeck, 'The Politics of Public Debt: Neoliberalism, Capitalist Development and the Restructuring of the State', *German Economic Review* 15.1 (2013), pp. 143–65, esp. p. 155. Italics in original. Cf. Robert Brenner, *The Economics of Global Turbulence*, *New Left Review* I/229 (special issue).

13 Geoff Mann and Joel Wainwright, *Climate Leviathan* (London, 2017), p. 34, n. 27.

14 See Jeremy Green, *Is Globalization Over?* (Oxford, 2019); and Adam Tooze, 'Who is Afraid of Inflation? The Long Shadow of the 1970s', *Journal of Modern European History* 12.1 (2014), pp. 53–60.

15 Cf. Banning Garrett, 'How Technology Is Driving Us Towards Peak Globalization', *SingularityHub*: https://singularityhub.com/2017/10/22/peak-globalization-is-the-path-to-a-sustainable-economy/.

16 Lisa Garforth, *Green Utopias: Environmental Hope Before and After Nature* (Oxford, 2017), esp. ch. 6.

17 Fred Hirsch, *Social Limits to Growth* (London, 1977), pp. 96f.

18 Ibid., p. 101.

19 Cf. Oliver James, *Affluenza* (London, 2007). Michel Foucault, *The History of Sexuality*, 3 vols (London, 1989); the long-awaited fourth volume has just been published in French as *Les aveux de la chair* (Paris, 2018).

20 Martin Gilens and Benjamin Page, *Democracy in America? What Has Gone Wrong and What We Can Do About It*

(Chicago, 2018), esp. ch. 2; Piketty, *Capital in the Twenty-First Century*, pp. 358, 464.

21 Hirsch, *Social Limits to Growth*, p. 190.

22 For a brilliant conceptual history, see Fredrik Albritton-Jonsson, 'The Origins of Cornucopianism: A Preliminary Genealogy', *Critical Historical Studies* 1.1 (2014), pp. 151–68.

23 Colin Crouch, 'Privatized Keynesianism: An Unacknowledged Policy Regime', *British Journal of Politics and International Relations* 11 (2009), pp. 382–99; and *The Strange Non-Death of Neoliberalism* (Oxford, 2015).

24 For the broader political and cultural contexts of American oil politics, see Meg Jacobs, *Panic at the Pump: The Energy Crisis and the Transformation of American Politics in the 1970s* (New York, 2017).

25 Hirsch, *Social Limits to Growth*, p. 17.

26 Donella H. Meadows, Dennis L. Meadows, Jørgen Randers and William W. Behrens III, *The Limits to Growth: A Report for the Club of Rome's Project on the Predicament of Mankind* (New York, 1972), p. 27.

27 Ibid., p. 23.

28 Ibid., p. 34; cf. Danny Dorling, *Population 10 Billion* (London, 2013).

29 Meadows et al., *Limits to Growth*, p. 183.

30 Donella H. Meadows, Dennis L. Meadows and Jørgen Randers, *Limits to Growth: The 30-Year Update* (London, 2004), pp. xvi, xv.

31 Cf. Arne Naess, *Ecology, Community and Lifestyle* (Cambridge, 1989); and James Robertson, *Future Work* (New York, 1985).

32 Cf. Paul Ehrlich, *The Population Bomb* (New York, 1969).

33 Karl S. Zimmerer, 'Human Geography and the New Ecology', *Annals of the American Society of Geographers* 84.1 (1994), pp. 108–25.

34 Thomas Robertson, *The Malthusian Moment: Global Population Growth and the Birth of American Environmentalism* (New Brunswick, NJ, 2012), esp. pp. 128–32.

35 See Jay W. Forrester, *World Dynamics* (Cambridge, 1972); and Chris Freeman, 'Malthus with a Computer', in H. S. D. Cole, Christopher Freeman, Marie Jahoda and K. L. R. Poritt (eds), *Thinking about the Future: A Critique of the Limits to Growth* (London, 1973), pp. 5–13. See also H. S. D. Cole, 'The Structure of the World Models', ibid., pp. 14–32. Nigel Calder, *Technopolis – Social Control of the Uses of Science* (London, 1970), esp. pp. 126–44, provides a different

political criticism of 'Fiction from Rome', concerning technological divides from Italy and Scandinavia to the United
States.
36 Robert Solow, 'Is the End of the World at Hand?' *Challenge*
16.1 (1973), pp. 39–50, at p. 48.
37 See Diane Coyle, *GDP – A Brief but Affectionate History*
(Princeton, NJ, 2015); cf. Partha Dasgupta, 'Wealth,
Well-Being and the Sustainable Development Goals', UNESCO
Well-Being Lecture (2014): http://mgiep.unesco.org/article/
wealth-well-being-and-the-sustainable-development-goals.
38 John Barry, 'Climate Change, "The Cancer State of Capitalism"
and the Return of Limits to Growth: Towards a Political
Economy of Sustainability', in Mark Pelling, David Mancel-
Naravette and Michael Redclift (eds), *Climate Change and the
Crisis of Capitalism* (London, 2012), pp. 129–42, at pp. 132,
136ff., 141.
39 Timothy Mitchell, 'Economentality: How the Future Entered
Government', *Critical Inquiry* 40.4 (2014), pp. 479–507.
40 Samuel Moyn, *Not Enough* (Cambridge, MA, 2018).
41 Jonsson, 'Cornucopianism', pp. 166ff.; cf. Wrigley, *Energy
and the Industrial Revolution*; Mauro Boianovsky and Kevin
D. Hoover, 'In the Kingdom of Solovia: The Rise of Growth
Economics at MIT, 1956–1970', *History of Political Economy*
46 (2014 Supplement), pp. 198–228.
42 Cf. Andrew Gamble, *Politics and Fate* (Oxford, 2009), pp.
100–4, 119f.; and David Runciman, 'Optimism, Pessimism and
Fatalism', in Forrester and Smith (eds), *Nature, Action and the
Future*, pp. 202–20.
43 On Adam Smith's rejection of the stationary state, see István
Hont, *The Politics of Commercial Society* (Cambridge, MA,
2016); on the Highlands as test case, see Fredrik Albritton-
Jonsson, *Enlightenment's Frontier* (New Haven, CT, 2013), esp.
pp. 260f.
44 Robert L. Heilbroner and Jack Allentuck, 'Ecological "Balance"
and the "Stationary State"', *Land Economics* 48.3 (1972), pp.
205–11, at pp. 209, 211.
45 Kenneth Boulding, 'The Shadow of the Stationary State',
Daedalus 102.4 (1973), pp. 89–101, at p. 90.
46 Cf. E. P. Thompson, 'Time, Work-Discipline, and Industrial
Capitalism', *Past and Present* 38 (1967), pp. 56–97; Vanessa
Ogle, *The Global Transformation of Time* (Cambridge, MA,
2015); and Sebastian Conrad, '"Nothing Is the Way It Should Be":
Global Transformations of the Time Regime in the Nineteenth
Century', *Modern Intellectual History* 15.3 (2018), pp. 821–48.

47 Tim Rogan, *The Moral Economists* (Princeton, NJ, 2018); cf. Tehila Sasson, 'The Gospel of Wealth', *Dissent* (22 August 2018): https://www.dissentmagazine.org/online_articles/tim-rogan-moral-economists-critique-capitalism-book-review.

48 Boulding, 'Shadow', p. 95.

49 Cf. István Hont, 'Adam Smith's History of Law and Government as Political Theory', in Richard Bourke and Raymond Geuss (eds), *Political Judgment* (Cambridge, 2009), pp. 131–71; and Paul Sagar, *The Opinion of Mankind* (Princeton, NJ, 2018).

50 Cf. Brian Barry, 'Circumstances of Justice and Future Generations', in R. I. Sikora and Brian Barry (eds), *Obligations to Future Generations* (Philadelphia, PA, 1978), for one attempt to render Rawls's nationally focused project into a stronger commitment to justice across wide generational gaps (and latterly towards global justice). On forms of universal basic income and models of growth, see Peter Sloman, 'Universal Basic Income in British Politics: From a "Vagabond's Wage" to a Global Debate', *Journal of Social Policy* 47.3 (2018), pp. 625–42.

51 James Meade, *Efficiency, Equality and the Ownership of Property* (London, 1964).

52 See Ben Jackson, 'Revisionism Reconsidered: "Property Owning Democracy" and Egalitarian Strategy in Post-War Britain', *Twentieth Century British History* 16.4 (2005), pp. 416–40, for Meade in particular. Meade was also exercised by pessimistic Malthusian fears about British political economy in the face of automation and population pressures (themes not directly taken up by Rawls).

53 P. MacKenzie Bok, 'To the Mountaintop, Again: The Early Rawls and Post-Protestant Ethics in Post-War America', *Modern Intellectual History* 14.1 (2017), pp. 153–85; and Katrina Forrester, 'Citizenship, War and the Origins of International Ethics in American Political Philosophy, 1960–1975', *Historical Journal* 57.3 (2014), pp. 773–801.

54 Cf. Calder, *Technopolis*, pp. 171–86, on contemporary challenges of thinking about a 'shared' environment.

55 Nicholas Georgescu-Roegen, *The Entropy Law and the Economic Process* (Cambridge, MA, 1971).

56 Nicholas Georgescu-Roegen, 'Energy and Economic Myths', *Southern Economic Journal*, 41.3 (1975), pp. 347–81, at p. 367.

57 Herman Daly, 'Ecologies of Scale', interview with Benjamin Kunkel, *New Left Review* 109 (2018), p. 88.

58 Gregory Claeys, *Mill on Paternalism* (Cambridge, 2016).

59 Boulding, 'Shadow', pp. 92ff.; for his attempt to integrate systems of social science to deal with system-wide challenges, see Phillipe Fontaine, 'Stabilizing American Society: Kenneth Boulding and the Integration of the Social Sciences', *Science in Context* 23.2 (2010), pp. 221–65.

60 Boulding, 'Shadow', p. 100.

61 Philip Mirowski, *More Heat than Light* (Cambridge, 1989); and Daniel Bell, *The Coming of Post-Industrial Society* (New York, 1976).

62 Paul Mason, *Post-Capitalism* (London, 2016); see also Robin Mackay and Armen Avanessian, *#Accelerationism: The Accelerationist Reader* (Falmouth, 2017). Yuval Harari, *Sapiens* (London, 2015). Cf. Publius Decius Mus, 'The Flight 93 Election', *Claremont Review of Books Digital* (5 September 2016): https://www.claremont.org/crb/basicpage/the-flight-93-election/.

63 Boris Fraenkel, *The Post-Industrial Utopians* (Oxford, 1987); cf. André Gorz, *Critique of Economic Reason* (London, 1989); and *Farewell to the Working Class* (London, 1982), p. 80.

64 See, for example, Hans Magnus Enzensberger, 'Critique of Political Ecology', in Ted Benton (ed.), *The Greening of Marxism* (New York, 1996), pp. 13–50, at p. 48.

65 Bertell Ollman and James Lawler (eds), *Market Socialism: The Debate Among Socialists* (London, 1998).

66 Giorgos Kallis, *Degrowth* (Ithaca, NY, 2018).

67 Troy Vettese, 'To Freeze the Thames', *New Left Review* 111 (2018), pp. 63–86, at pp. 65, 67.

68 E. O. Wilson, *Half-Earth: Our Planet's Fight for Life* (New York, 2017); cf. Robert Macfarlane, *The Wild Places* (London, 2017).

69 Cf. Isaac Nakhimovsky, *The Closed Commercial State* (Princeton, NJ, 2015).

70 China Miéville, 'The Limits of Utopia', *Salvage*: http://salvage.zone/in-print/the-limits-of-utopia/.

71 Dieter Helm, *The Carbon Crunch* (New Haven, CT, 2012), p. 234. Emphasis added.

72 Paul Krugman, 'Gambling with Civilization', *New York Review of Books* (7 November 2013): https://www.nybooks.com/articles/2013/11/07/climate-change-gambling-civilization/.

73 Helm, *Burnout*.

74 Krugman, 'Gambling with Civilization'.

75 Dieter Helm, *Natural Capital: Valuing the Planet* (New Haven, CT, 2015).

76 Krugman, 'Gambling'.

77 Cf. Richard Tuck, *Political Thought and the Rights of War and*

Peace (Oxford, 2001); and Martii Koskeniemmi, *The Gentle Civilizer of Nations* (Cambridge, 1993).

Chapter 4 Ecological Debts

1 John Brewer, *The Sinews of Power* (London, 1989).
2 István Hont, *Jealousy of Trade* (Cambridge, MA, 2010), ch. 4.
3 Dani Rodrik, *The Globalization Paradox* (Oxford, 2012).
4 Adam Tooze, *Crashed* (London, 2018), pp. 7–9.
5 Arthur Pigou, 'A Special Levy to Discharge War Debts', *Economic Journal* (June 1918), pp. 137ff., 142f.
6 Thomas Piketty, 'Our Manifesto is to Save Europe from Itself', *The Guardian* (9 December 2018): https:// www.theguardian.com/commentisfree/2018/dec/09/ manifesto-divided-europe-inequality-europeans.
7 Wolfgang Streeck, *Buying Time* (London, 2014); and *How Will Capitalism End?* (London, 2017).
8 Jason Moore, *Capitalism in the Web of Life: Ecology and the Accumulation of Capital* (London, 2015); Jason Moore (ed.), *Anthropocene or Capitalocene? Nature, History and the Crisis of Capitalism* (Oakland, CA, 2016).
9 Jason Moore and Raj Patel, *A History of the World in Seven Cheap Things: A Guide to Capitalism, Nature, and the Future of the Planet* (London, 2018), p. 21.
10 Ibid., pp. 46f.; cf. Silvia Federici, *Caliban and the Witch* (London, 2017).
11 Cf. James Walvin, *Sugar: The World Corrupted from Slavery to Obesity* (New York, 2018).
12 Cf. Geoffrey de Ste Croix, *The Class Struggle in the Ancient Greek World* (London, 1978).
13 Cf. Rob Nixon, *Slow Violence and the Environmentalism of the Poor* (Cambridge, MA, 2013); and John S. Dryzek, Richard B. Nordgard and David Schlosberg, *Climate-Challenged Society* (Oxford, 2013).
14 Moore and Patel, *History of the World*, p. 107.
15 Ibid., pp. 42f.
16 See Alasia Nuti, *Injustice and the Reproduction of History: Structural Inequalities, Gender and Redress* (Cambridge, 2019). Cf. Jeremy Waldron, 'Superseding Historic Injustice', *Ethics* 103.1 (1992), pp. 4–28. The irony for practising politicians trying to think about this is clearly seen when we recall Gordon Brown's proud announcement at the cancelling of $40bn of debt at Gleneagles in 2005, having apparently moved the economy

'beyond boom and bust', only to face the Great Recession of 2008.
17 Rebecca Willis, 'Constructing a "Representative Claim" for Action on Climate Change', *Political Studies*, 66.4 (2018), pp. 940–58.
18 Cf. Robert Nozick, *Anarchy, State and Utopia* (New York, 1974); G. A. Cohen, *Self-Ownership, Freedom and Equality* (Cambridge, 1985); and John Rawls, *The Law of Peoples* (Cambridge, MA, 1999).
19 Christian Baatz, 'Responsibility for the Past? Some Thoughts on Compensating Those Vulnerable to Climate Change in Developing Countries', *Ethics, Policy and Environment* 16.1 (2013), pp. 94–110.
20 Fredric Jameson, 'Future City', *New Left Review* 21 (2003), pp. 65–79, at p. 67. Jameson wrote of this phrase that 'someone once said this', before making his own argument about history and catastrophe. In debates as to its origin, most point to Slavoj Žižek or J. G. Ballard.
21 Michael Hardt and Antonio Negri, *Assembly* (Oxford, 2017).
22 J. M. Keynes, 'National Self-Sufficiency', *Collected Works*, XXI, *Activities, 1931–1939* (Cambridge, 1989), pp. 233–46.
23 Mann and Wainwright, *Climate Leviathan*, pp. 15, 23, 26, 31.
24 Lonnie G. Thompson, 'Climate Change: The Evidence and Our Options', *Behavioural Analysis* 33.2 (2010), pp. 153–70.
25 Mann and Wainwright, *Climate Leviathan*, pp. 54ff.
26 Compare https://19january2017snapshot.epa.gov/ and https://www.epa.gov/.
27 For one classic left-wing illustration, see Georg Lukács, *History and Class Consciousness*, trans. R. Merlin (London, 1971).
28 Bernard Williams, *Truth and Truthfulness* (Princeton, NJ, 2006); and Miranda Fricker, *Epistemic Injustice* (Oxford, 2009).
29 Jason Moore, '"Amsterdam is Standing on Norway" Part I: The Alchemy of Capital, Empire and Nature in the Diaspora of Wilver, 1545–1648', *Journal of Agrarian Change* 10.1 (2010), pp. 33–68; and '"Amsterdam is Standing on Norway" Part II: The Global North Atlantic in the Ecological Revolution of the Long Seventeenth Century', *Journal of Agrarian Change* 10.2 (2010), pp. 188–227.
30 https://www.hollandersvandegoudeneeuw.nl/en.
31 Jonathan Israel, *The Dutch Republic – Its Rise, Greatness, and Fall* (Oxford, 1998).
32 Warde, *Invention of Sustainability*, ch. 7.
33 Elizabeth Kolberg, 'Greenland is Melting', *New Yorker* (24 October 2016): https://www.newyorker.com/magazine/2016/

10/24/greenland-is-melting. Cf. her 'How to Write About a Vanishing World', *New Yorker* (15 October 2018): https://www.newyorker.com/magazine/2018/10/15/how-to-write-about-a-vanishing-world.

34 Crutzen, 'Geology of Mankind'.

35 H. Damon Matthews, 'Quantifying Historical Carbon and Climate Debts among Nations', *Nature Climate Change* 6 (January 2016), pp. 60–4, at p. 60.

36 Henry Shue, *Climate Justice* (Oxford, 2016).

37 Donald Mackenzie, 'Making Things the Same: Gases, Emission Rights and the Politics of Carbon Markets', *Accounting, Organizations and Society* 34 (2009), pp. 440–55.

38 Hanna Beech, '"We Cannot Afford This": Malaysia Pushes Back Against China's Vision', *New York Times* (20 August 2018): https://www.nytimes.com/2018/08/20/world/asia/china-malaysia.html?hp&action=click&pgtype=Homepage&clickSource=story-heading&module=first-column-region&region=top-news&WT.nav=top-news.

39 Yannis Varoufakis, *Adults in the Room* (London, 2017); 'Greece Was Never Bailed Out – It Remains Locked in an EU Debtor's Prison, *The Guardian* (26 August 2018): https://www.theguardian.com/commentisfree/2018/aug/26/greece-was-never-bailed-out---it-remains-a-debtors-prison-and-the-eu-still-holds-the-keys.

40 Samuel Moyn, *Not Enough* (Cambridge, MA, 2018); Vijay Prashad, *The Darker Nations* (New York, 2008); and Gary Wilder, *Freedom Time* (Durham, NC, 2015). Cf. Brian Barry, *Rich Countries and Poor Countries* (1980): https://sites.google.com/a/york.ac.uk/brianbarryarchive/unpublished#FT.

41 James M. Robertson, 'Navigating the Postwar Liberal Order: Autonomy, Creativity and Modernism in Socialist Yugoslavia, 1949–1953', *Modern Intellectual History* (2018): https://doi.org/10/1017/S14792443180000379.

42 Malcolm Bull, 'Slack', in Forrester and Smith (eds), *Nature, Action and the Future*, pp. 94–112, at p. 111.

43 See Rikard Warlenius, Gregory Pierce and Vasna Ramasar, 'Reversing the Arrow of Arrears – The Concept of "Ecological Debt" and Its Value for Environmental Justice', *Global Environmental Change* 30 (2015), pp. 21–30, at p. 22.

44 Simon Caney, 'Climate Change, Human Rights, and Moral Thresholds', in Stephen Gardiner, Simon Caney, Dale Jamieson and Henry Shue (eds), *Climate Ethics* (Oxford, 2010), pp. 163–80.

45 Cf. Robert A. Klein, *Sovereign Equality Among States* (Toronto,

1974); and Ayse Zarakol, 'Sovereign Equality as Misrecognition', *Review of International Studies* 44.5 (2018), pp. 848–62.

46 See Joan Martinez-Alier, 'The Ecological Debt', *Kurswechsel* 4 (2002), pp. 5–16; and Andrew Simms, *Ecological Debt: Global Warming and the Wealth of Nations* (London, 2009).

47 Richard Tuck, 'Democracy and Terrorism', in Bourke and Geuss (eds), *Political Judgment*, pp. 313–32.

48 Will Potter, *Green is the New Red* (San Francisco, 2011).

49 Michael J. Lynch, Michael A. Long, Kimberly L. Barrett and Paul B. Stretesky, 'Is it a Crime to Produce Ecological Disorganization? Why Green Criminology and Political Economy Matter in the Analysis of Global Ecological Harms', *The British Journal of Criminology* 53.6 (2013), pp. 997–1016.

50 Nietzsche, *Genealogy of Morality*, II.13: 'only something which has no history can be defined'.

51 See R. H. Lossin, 'Sabotage as Political Activism', *Public Seminar* (3 July 2018): http://www.publicseminar.org/2018/07/sabotage-as-environmental-activism/.

52 Volkan S. Ediger and John V. Bowlus, 'A Farewell to King Coal: Geopolitics, Energy Security and the Transition to Oil, 1898–1917', *Historical Journal*: https://doi:10.1017/S0018246X180000109.

53 Mitchell, *Carbon Democracy*.

54 Solow, 'End of the World', p. 50.

Chapter 5 Population Futures

1 Diana Coole, *Should We Limit World Population?* (Oxford, 2018).

2 Melinda Cooper, *Family Values: Between Neoliberalism and Social Conservatism* (Cambridge, MA, 2017). As evangelical Christians worried about this, lawyers were also writing, in deeply historical terms, about how the history of rights ascribed to non-human persons (states, corporations, etc.) stemmed from a long history of gradually sorting out what had once seemed 'unthinkable'. Ascribing legal rights to nature could therefore be just another way-station along this road. See Christopher D. Stone, *Should Trees Have Standing?* (Los Altos, CA, 1974), pp. 454f., 464.

3 Nathaniel Rich, 'Losing Earth: The Decade We Almost Stopped Climate Change', *New York Times Magazine* (1 August 2018): https://www.nytimes.com/interactive/2018/08/01/magazine/climate-change-losing-earth.html.

4 Cf. Purdy, *After Nature*.
5 J. R. McNeill and Peter Engelke, *The Great Acceleration* (Cambridge, MA, 2016), pp. 38ff., 41, 64.
6 Bashford, *Global Population*, chs 1–2.
7 Cf. James C. Scott, *Seeing Like a State* (New Haven, CT, 1999); *Against the Grain* (New Haven, CT, 2017); John F. Haldon, *The State and the Tributary Mode of Production* (London, 1994); and Mark Harrison, 'The Peasant Mode of Production in the Work of A. V. Chayanov', *Journal of Peasant Studies* 4.4. (1977), pp. 323–36.
8 For hints in this direction, see Perry Anderson, *English Questions* (London, 1992).
9 Garrett Hardin, 'The Tragedy of the Commons', *Science* (13 December 1968), pp. 1243–8; and 'Living on a Lifeboat', *Bioscience* 24.10 (1974), pp. 561–8.
10 For an overview, see Elinor Ostrom, 'Converting Threats into Opportunities', *PS: Political Science and Politics* 39.1 (2006), pp. 3–12.
11 Charles Kolstad et al., 'Social, Economic and Ethical Concepts and Methods', in Ottmar Edenhoffer et al., *Climate Change 2014: Mitigation of Climate Change. Contribution of Working Group III to the Fifth Assessment Report of the Intergovernmental Panel on Climate Change* (Cambridge, 2014), pp. 207–82, at pp. 223f.
12 John Broome, *Counting the Cost of Global Warming* (Cambridge, 1992), pp. 49, 115–22.
13 See Michel Foucault, *Security, Territory and Population*, ed. M. Senellart, trans. G. Burchell (Basingstoke, 2007).
14 Diana Coole, 'Too Many Bodies? The Return and Disavowal of the Population Question', *Environmental Politics* 22.2 (2013), pp. 195–215, at p. 196.
15 Onora Nell, 'Lifeboat Earth', *Philosophy and Public Affairs* 4.3 (1975), pp. 273–92.
16 Samuel Moyn, *Christian Human Rights* (Philadelphia, PA, 2015); and Marco Duranti, *The Conservative Human Rights Revolution* (Oxford, 2017).
17 For liberal philosophical debates on these subjects, compare David Miller, *Strangers in Our Midst* (Cambridge, MA, 2018); Arash Abizadeh, 'Democratic Theory and Border Coercion: No Right to Unilaterally Control Your Own Borders', *Political Theory* 36.1 (2008), pp. 37–65; Lea Ypi, 'What's Wrong With Colonialism', *Philosophy and Public Affairs* 41.2 (2013), pp. 158–91; and Kieran Oberman, 'Poverty and Immigration Policy', *American Political Science Review* 109.2 (2015), pp. 239–51.

18 Andreas Malm, *The Progress of This Storm* (London, 2018); Timothy Shenk, 'Is Democracy Dying?', *The New Republic* (20 August 2018); and John Thompson, *Political Scandal* (Oxford, 2000).

19 For the history of this evolution, see Hont, *Jealousy of Trade*, ch. 5; for an interesting development of the theme, see J. G. A. Pocock, 'The Nation State as Historical Critique', in Béla Kapossy, Isaac Nakhimovsky, Sophus Reinert and Richard Whatmore (eds), *Markets, Morals, Politics* (Cambridge, MA, 2017), pp. 265–84.

20 Olaf Corry, 'Globalising the Arctic Climate: Geoengineering and the Emerging Global Polity', in Kathrin Keil and Sebastian Knecht (eds), *Governing Arctic Change: Global Perspectives* (Basingstoke, 2016), pp. 59–78.

21 Walter Benjamin, 'Theses on the Philosophy of History', in *Illuminations*, trans. H. Zohn (London, 1973), pp. 245–55, esp. p. 249.

22 Cf. Christopher H. Achens and Larry Bartels, *Democracy for Realists* (Princeton, NJ, 2017); and Alison McQueen, *Political Realism in Apocalyptic Times* (Cambridge, 2018).

23 Particularly important here was the work of Stuart Hall and Edward Said on 'articulations' of hegemony, and on the ways in which various cultures (particularly the Palestinian) were continuously 'negated' as legitimate identities by the unspoken assumptions of Orientalism. Cf. Stuart Hall, *Selected Political Writings* (Durham, NC, 2017); and Edward Said, *Orientalism* (London, 2003).

24 See Warren Breckman, *Post-Marxism* (Ithaca, NY, 2013).

25 Cf. John Dunn, *Setting the People Free*, 2nd edition (Princeton, NJ, 2018).

26 Rudolf Bahro, *From Red to Green* (London, 1984); John Bellamy Foster and Brett Clark, *The Ecological Rift: Capitalism's War on Earth* (New York, 2013); cf. Michel Foucault, *Society Must Be Defended*, ed. A. Fontana, trans. D. Macey (Basingstoke, 2003).

27 Jan Narveson, 'Moral Problems of Population', *Monist* 57.1 (1973), pp. 62–86, at p. 80.

28 John Broome, 'Should We Value Population?', *Journal of Political Philosophy* 13.4 (2005), pp. 399–413, at pp. 410f.

29 Cf. Derek Parfit, 'Equality or Priority', *Ratio* 10.3 (1997), pp. 202–21; and 'Can We Avoid the Repugnant Conclusion?' *Theoria* 82 (2016), pp. 110–27. For discussion, Martin O'Neill, 'What Should Egalitarians Believe?' *Philosophy and Public Affairs* 36.2 (2008), pp. 119–56. On ancient sorites paradoxes, see R. M. Sainsbury, *Paradoxes* (Cambridge, 1995).

30 Partha Dasgupta and Eric Maskin, 'Uncertainty and Hyperbolic Discounting', *American Economic Review* 95.4 (2005), pp. 1290–9.
31 Nicholas Stern, *The Economics of Climate Change: The Stern Review* (Cambridge, 2007).
32 William Deringer, 'Pricing the Future in the Seventeenth Century: Calculating Technologies in Competition', *Technology and Culture* 58.2 (2017), pp. 506–28.
33 Kenneth Arrow et al., 'Sustainability and the Measurement of Wealth: Further Reflections', *Environment and Development Economics* 18 (2013), pp. 504–16.
34 Cf. Melissa Lane, 'Uncertainty, Action and Politics: The Problem of Negligibility', in Forrester and Smith (eds), *Nature, Action and the Future*, pp. 157–79, at pp. 177f., where it becomes the 'false freezing of the fundamental conditions of politics'. Cf. Richard Tuck, 'Negligibility: A Response to Melissa Lane', in ibid., pp. 180–201, at pp. 189–92, 196–200.

Chapter 6 Value

1 See Partha Dasgupta, 'Inclusive National Accounts', *SANDEE* Working Paper (January 2012), p. 14.
2 It might also connect to the idea of 'ghost acreage' and 'environmental space' as considered by Georg Borogström, on which see Warlenius et al., 'Reversing the Arrow', pp. 25f.
3 Amartya Sen, *Development as Freedom* (Oxford, 2001).
4 For instance, Leif Wenar, *Blood Oil* (Oxford, 2015).
5 George Monbiot, *Out of This Wreckage* (London, 2017).
6 Harry Frankfurt, *The Importance of What We Care About* (Cambridge, 1998), esp. ch. 2.
7 For a related discussion, see Duncan Kelly, *The Propriety of Liberty* (Princeton, NJ, 2011), pp. 270ff.
8 Miéville, 'Limits of Utopia'.
9 On this work in progress, see the discussion by Robinson Meyer, 'The Democratic Party Wants to Make Climate Policy Exciting', *The Atlantic* (5 December 2018): https://www.theatlantic.com/science/archive/2018/12/ocasio-cortez-green-new-deal-winning-climate-strategy/576514/. Cf. New Economic Foundation, *A Green New Deal* (London, 2008): https://neweconomics.org/uploads/files/8f737ea195fe56db2f_xbm6ihwb1.pdf.
10 Roy Scranton, *Learning to Die in the Anthropocene* (San Francisco, 2015).
11 See the classic essay by J. G. A. Pocock, 'Time, History and

Eschatology in the Thought of Thomas Hobbes', in *Politics, Language and Time* (Chicago, 1989), pp. 148–201.

12 Stone, *Should Trees Have Standing?*, p. 464.

13 Timothy Clark, 'What on World is the Earth? The Anthropocene and Fictions of the Earth', *Oxford Literary Review* 35.1 (2013), pp. 5–24, at pp. 9f.

14 Clive Hamilton, *Defiant Earth: The Fate of Humans in the Anthropocene* (Oxford, 2017), pp. 19, 41ff., 63, 155.

15 Ben Lazier, 'Earthrise: or, The Globalization of the World Picture', *American Historical Review* 116.3 (2011), pp. 602–30.

16 Bruno Latour, *Facing Gaia*, trans. C. Porter (Cambridge, 2018), pp. 125, 128ff., 136–9; and 'Agency at the Time of the Anthropocene', *New Literary History* 45.1 (2014), pp. 1–18.

17 Latour, *Facing Gaia*, pp. 238, 248.

18 Bruno Latour, *Down to Earth*, trans. C. Porter (Cambridge, 2018), pp. 44, 41, 37, 56.

19 Cf. John Dryzek, 'The Forum, the System and the Polity: Three Varieties of Democratic Theory', *Political Theory* 45.5 (2017), pp. 610–36.

20 Cf. Alyssa Battistoni, 'Bringing in the Work of Nature: From Natural Capital to Hybrid Labour', *Political Theory* 45.1 (2017), pp. 5–31; Andrea Sangiovanni, 'Solidarity in the European Union', *Oxford Journal of Legal Studies* 33.2 (2013), pp. 213–41.

21 Donna Haraway, *Staying with the Trouble* (Durham, NC, 2016), pp. 13ff., 31ff.

22 Ibid., pp. 104ff.

23 Ibid., p. 108; cf. Oliver Sacks, *The Man Who Mistook His Wife for a Hat* (London, 2011); and Henry Marsh, *Do No Harm* (London, 2014).

24 Jane Bennett, *Vibrant Matter* (Durham, NC, 2010).

25 Ian Hacking, 'Kinds of People: Moving Targets', *Proceedings of the British Academy* 151 (2007), pp. 285–318; 'Making up People', *London Review of Books* 28.16 (17 August 2006), pp. 23–6.

26 See Barbara Ward and René Dubos, *Only One Earth* (New York, 1983).

27 Andreas Malm and Alf Hornborg, 'The Geology of Mankind? A Critique of the Anthropocene Narrative', *The Anthropocene Review* 1.1 (2014), pp. 62–9.

28 Amitav Ghosh, *The Great Derangement* (Chicago, 2016). For a sympathetic review, see Fredrik Albritton-Jonsson, 'The Holocene Hangover: It Is Time for Humanity to Make Fundamental Changes', *The Guardian* (7 December 2016): https://www.

theguardian.com/books/2016/dec/07/the-holocene-hangover-it-is-time-for-humanity-to-make-fundamental-changes.

29 For example, Mark Lilla, 'Two Roads for the New French Right', *New York Review of Books* (20 December 2018).

30 Mark Blyth, *Austerity: The History of a Dangerous Idea* (Oxford, 2015).

31 Dipesh Chakrabarty, *The Crises of Civilization: Exploring Global and Planetary Histories* (Oxford, 2019).

32 Deborah R. Coen, *Climate in Motion: Science, Empire, and the Problem of Scale* (Chicago, 2018).

Epilogue: Historical Possibilities for an Anthropocened Politics

1 John Dunn, 'The History of Political Theory', in *The History of Political Theory and Other Essays* (Cambridge, 1996), pp. 11–38, esp. pp. 13, 24ff.; and Terence Ball, James Farr and Russell L. Hanson (eds), *Political Innovation and Conceptual Change* (Cambridge, 1989).

2 Andrew Revkin, 'Confronting the Anthropocene', *New York Times* (11 May 2011): https://dotearth.blogs.nytimes.com/2011/05/11/confronting-the-anthropocene/.

3 Stephen Gardiner, 'Climate Change Ethics in a Dark and Dangerous Time', *Ethics* 127 (2017), pp. 430–65, at p. 436.

4 Dale Jamieson, 'Ethics, Public Policy, and Global Warming', in Gardiner et al. (eds), *Climate Ethics*, pp. 77–86.

5 Tim Hayward, *Political Theory and Ecological Values* (Oxford, 1998), pp. 54f., 79, 88.

6 Robyn Eckersley, *Environmentalism and Political Theory* (London, 1997), pp. 154ff., 179.

7 UNDP Report, New Directions of Human Security (1994), http://hdr.undp.org/en/content/human-development-report-1994. See, more recently, Leigh Johnson, 'Geographies of Securitized Catastrophe Risk and the Implications of Climate Change', *Economic Geography* 90.2 (2014), pp. 155–85; and David Nally, 'Governing Precarious Lives: Land Grabs, Geopolitics, and "Food Security"', *The Geographical Journal* 181.4 (2015), pp. 340–9.

8 For a sympathetic overview, see Simon Caney, 'Climate Change, Human Rights and Moral Thresholds', in Gardiner et al. (eds), *Climate Ethics*, pp. 163–77; the source here is Henry Shue, *Basic Rights* (Oxford, 1977); cf. Patrick Sharma, *Robert McNamara's Other War* (University Park, PA, 2017).

9 Cf. John Dunn, 'Why We Need a Global History of Political Thought', in Kapossy et al. (eds), *Markets, Morals, Politics*, pp. 285–310.

10 Cf. Bob Jessop, 'Nicos Poulantzas on Political Economy, Political Ecology, and Democratic Socialism', *Journal of Political Ecology* 24.1 (2017), pp. 186–99.

11 Elizabeth Anderson, 'What's the Point of Equality?', *Ethics* 10.2 (1999), pp. 287–337.

12 Mette Eilstrup-Sangiovanni, 'Why the World Needs an International Cyberwar Convention', *Philosophy and Technology* 31.3 (2018), pp. 379–407.

13 Latour, *Down to Earth*, pp. 86, 90. Sophia Rosenfeld, *Democracy and Truth* (University Park, PA, 2018).

14 Latour, *Down to Earth*, pp. 98–101.

15 Jürgen Habermas, *Europe: The Faltering Project*, trans. C. Cronin (Oxford, 2009); and *The Crisis of the European Union: A Response*, trans. C. Cronin (Oxford, 2012), pp. 11, 21–5, 32f. and 35. More broadly, see Jan Werner Müller, *Constitutional Patriotism* (Princeton, NJ, 2007).

16 David N. Livingstone, 'The Climate of War: Violence, Warfare, and Climatic Reductionism', *WIREs Climate Change* 6 (2015), pp. 437–44.

17 Paul Schnarre, 'Robotics on the Battlefield II: The Coming Swarm', *CNAS* (2014): https://s3.amazonaws.com/files.cnas.org/documents/CNAS_TheComingSwarm_Scharre.pdf.

Index